The Iron Cross

THE IRON CROSS

A History 1813–1957

GORDON WILLIAMSON

BLANDFORD PRESS
POOLE · DORSET

To my wife Marilyn

Frontispiece
Crown Prince Albert Friedrich Augustus of Saxony, holder of the Grand Cross of 1870 and the *Pour le Mérire.*

First published in the UK 1984 by Blandford Press,
Link House, West Street, Poole, Dorset BH15 1LL

Reprinted 1985

British Library Cataloguing in Publication Data

Williamson, Gordon
The Iron Cross.
1. Iron Cross—History
I. Title
355.1'342 CR5351

ISBN 0 7137 1460 3

Typeset by Graphicraft Typesetters Limited Hong Kong.
Printed in Great Britain by
Richard Clay (The Chaucer Press) Ltd,
Bungay, Suffolk

CONTENTS

FOREWORD

The visit of the young author, Gordon Williamson, to West Germany during the spring of 1982 gave me the opportunity to study the manuscript of his book *The Iron Cross* and also made it possible for me to introduce him and his work to the Ordensgemeinschaft der Ritterkreuzträger (Landesgruppe Nord).

The meeting of such a young Briton, who has studied a part of modern German history with great determination, and about forty ex-officers of both World Wars was a special experience for all of us. I think this meeting made all participants deeply conscious of the fact that the nations of Western Europe fought each other in bitter and bloody battles until the end of World War Two, instead of protecting their rich cultures and preserving their heritages.

I experienced the biggest airborne operation of World War Two at Arnhem as First Ordnance Officer to Generalfeldmarschall Walter Model, and can say that everybody fought with great gallantry. After several days of heavy fighting, both sides agreed to a brief cease-fire of a few hours to retrieve the wounded and dead. That was an act of chivalry and true humanity which soldiers will never forget. In addition to a high regard for the brave enemy, I seem to have recognized a deep compassion and sympathy on the faces of individual soldiers. Today, forty years later, the people of Western Europe, and their allies, should understand that they have a great common responsibility in keeping peace in the world, and peace *with* freedom.

And now to the message of this book, as I see it. The Iron Cross was instituted by the King of Prussia, Friedrich Wilhelm III on 10 March 1813, the birthday of his Queen, Louise. Prussia was at that time trying to recover from war and at the same time throw off the oppression of Napoleon. Self sacrifice, courage and bravery in the quest for freedom were to be recognized by the award of this Iron Cross.

As Germans, we are thankful to Gordon Williamson who, as a young author, has studied the 170-year history of the Iron Cross. In Britain, consciousness of history and tradition are taken for granted, but Germany seems to have surrendered to the erosion of its culture. The nations of the West, especially Germany, need good examples of tradition and culture from history as arms against the aggressive politics of terrorism and oppression. Many good examples from the history of German military tradition are given in this book, which should be interesting for British as well as for German readers.

I should like to close with a word from Feldmarschall Graf Neithardt von Gneisenau, who participated with Feldmarschall Blücher in the defeat of Napoleon at the Battle of Waterloo on 18 June 1815:

> We can only find our salvation in our determination, — and there are times in the histories of nations, where only the highest courage can save the situation.

Oelixdorf, 12 September 1983

HEINRICH SPRINGER,
Former SS-Sturmbannführer and
First Ordnance Officer on the staff of
Generalfeldmarschall Walter Model

ACKNOWLEDGEMENTS

The production of this work would not have been possible without the assistance of a number of contributors. It was their help, encouragement and vital contributions which brought about this book as the end product of what had originally been a purely private research project for my own satisfaction.

Peter Groch of West Berlin welcomed my wife and me to his home and took time off to show us the sights of that magnificent city. Additionally, he allowed me to photograph some of the rare Imperial Iron Crosses in his superb collection.

David Littlejohn of Aberdeen, Grampian, Scotland, an accomplished authority on the Third Reich period, and author of several reference works, has given much help and encouragement on this and other projects over the years.

Brian L Davis of South Croydon, Surrey, England, a respected authority on military uniforms and insignia and technical advisor to numerous film and television projects, has freely given much advice and assistance and allowed me the use of some fine photographs from his excellent collection.

Jak P Mallmann Showell of Telford, England, with whom I have had the pleasure of co-operating in the past, has been a constant source of encouragement and has allowed the use of several of his photographs. Jak's father was Dieselobermaschinist on *U-377* and won both First and Second Class Iron Crosses before being killed in action.

Chris Ailsby from Peterborough, Cambridgeshire, England, has, in the short space of time I have known him, provided me with some really exceptional photographic material, and this help is gratefully acknowledged.

Richard Schulze-Kossens, former Leibstandarte officer, and one time adjutant to Adolf Hitler, took time off from his busy schedule to meet me during my trip to Germany in 1982, and provided me with many excellent photographs.

My good friend Heinrich Springer of Oelixdorf, West Germany has been an enormous help. A Ritterkreuzträger and veteran of the elite Leibstandarte, Heinrich welcomed me to his home in summer 1982 and provided me with a wealth of information and photographic material. The hospitality shown to me by Heinrich and his charming wife Ursula made my trip immensely pleasurable as well as fruitful.

Thanks also to Michael and Scarlett Courtney, photographers, of Edinburgh for all their assistance.

A large number of other collectors and enthusiasts as well as German veterans immediately came forward and offered their assistance. I am happy now to acknowledge their help: Tom Archibald; Mike Bassett; Richard Baumgartner; Roger James Bender; Malcolm Bowers; Colin Brown; Barry Byrne; Bruce Cazels; Otto Engel; Peter Huckstepp; Dr K G Klietmann; Heinz Macher; Johannes Mühlenkamp; Eric Nichols; Anthony Prowse; Daniel Rose; Adolf Schmahl; Adalbert Schnee; Remy Schrijnen; John Shaw; Tim Stannard; Frederick J Stephens; Dr Phil Ernst Thomsen; Otto Weidinger.

Anthony Prowse is to be specially thanked for supplying a vast amount of reference material and allowing me to quote information from his book *The Iron Cross of Prussia and Germany.*

PICTURE CREDITS

(By page; T: top; B: bottom; C: centre; R: right; L: left.) C J Ailsby Collection: 50; 72; 73L, R; 77B; 92B; 107; 109B; 121T, C; 125; 131L, R; 147; 149L, R; 151TL, TR, B. T W Archibald: 117R; 133. Mike Bassett: 102; 104. R A Baumgartner: 48B; 53TL, TR. R J Bender: 78; 129. Dr Wolf-Heinrich Bleichrodt: 135. Heinrich Böhm: 80B. M Bowers Collection: 89BL, BR. C K Brown Collection: 122B. Barry Byrne: 117L; 126. Bruce Cazel: 50TL, TR; 51BL, BR. A W Charlton: 11B; 45T; 77T; 88L; 109T; 118; 156L; 157TL, B; 160B. Brian L Davis: 79; 111T, BL, BR. Otto Engel: 112T. Forman Piccadilly Ltd: 152L; 150. Otto Giese/Jak P Mallmann Showell: 70. Peter Groch Collection: 18C, B; 35; 36; 57T, B; 55. D Littlejohn: 122T. Dr K G Klietmann: 40TL. Kunst im Dritten Reich: 151B. Ronald Kwan Collection via F J Stephens: 154T. P J Huckstepp: 165. Institut für wissenschaftliche Ordenskunde, Berlin: 20; 24; 26; 27B; 29; 30; 39; 40TR, B; 41BL, BR; 42TL, TR, BL; 43; 58; 61; 61R. Heinz Macher: 64. Jak P Mallmann Showell: 80T; 81; 82; 83; 84; 85; 115; 116; 119T; 120; 161L, R; 162TL, TR, B; 163R, L. General Matzky: 157TR. M & T Militaria: 91L, R. Johannes Mühlenkamp: 119B. A E Prowse: 13B; 95. Daniel Rose Collection: 105BL, BR; 106T, BL, BR. Hans-Ulrich Rudel/C J Ailsby: 146. Adolf Schmahl: 110. Remi Schrijmen/C J Ailsby: 112B. Richard Schulze-Kossens: 86L, R; 87; 143. J Shaw Collection: 16TL, TR; 33; 37; 47BR; 159R; 160TL. Heinrich Springer: 98; 99; 101; 103; 105T; 139. T J Stannard Collection: 114T, B. F T Stephens: 108. Ernst-Heinrich Thomsen: 113. US Army via F J Stephens: 153. Otto Weidinger: 127.

INTRODUCTION

In the history of military decorations, few can have had the enormous impact of Germany's Iron Cross. Originally a purely Prussian award, it was instituted at a time when most of Europe was under Napoleonic domination, and it came to symbolise Prussia's determination for freedom. Assimilated into just about every aspect of German culture, the Iron Cross became more than just a military award. Today, a collector can find the Iron Cross motif emblazoned on virtually any type of artefact, including pottery, jewellery, banners, matchbox holders, and watch fobs, and even incorporated into the national flag itself. Even now, the armed forces of the West German Federal Republic use the Iron Cross motif as the national emblem borne by military aircraft and vehicles.

The Iron Cross has come full circle from its origins when Britain and Prussia stood as allies against Napoleon. Now, once again, the two nations are staunch allies in NATO, and, aptly, the new design of the Iron Cross closely resembles its 1813 predecessor.

The history of the Iron Cross is as extensive as it is fascinating and to cover it in depth would take a work of many volumes. It is hoped, however, that this book will give the reader a good insight into the rich history of one of the world's most famous awards, drawing as it does on many personal memories of surviving German veterans who graciously provided much information and photographic material from their personal albums. Access was also provided to original examples of almost every type of Iron Cross for examination and photographing.

Opposite above
The Iron Cross 2nd Class being worn immediately after the award. Note the method of tying the ribbon through the buttonhole.

Opposite
Iron Crosses through the ages, from left to right: the original 1813 design; the 1914 obverse; the 1939 obverse, and the 1957 version obverse.

THE IRON CROSS OF 1813

Following defeat at the hands of Napoleon in 1807, Prussia entered an era of humiliating subservience to the French. The King's hesitative and indecisive attitude had restricted the freedom of action of his Generals to such an extent that defeat had become inevitable. Now Prussia was to suffer the indignity of occupation by the French, with all the looting and pillaging which that occupation entailed.

Prussia's military leaders, unlike the King and his advisors, were still anxious to resist the French, and plotted insurrection. The Queen had a good deal of sympathy with them and was infuriated by her country's humiliation, but the weak willed King would not dare incur Napoleon's wrath by openly opposing him.

By 1808, however, military and social reforms in Prussia had laid the foundations for the successful rebuilding of Prussian power. The officer corps, once the domain of the rich and powerful, was opened to all with real ability. Corporal punishment, until then hideously harsh for even the slightest infringement, was abolished. (It is worth noting that Germany's greatest soldier of this era, Feldmarschall Gebhard Leberecht von Blücher, had already introduced these reforms into his Hussar Regiment some time earlier.) National Service was also introduced to provide the nation with a reserve of trained soldiery.

In 1809, Archduke Charles of Austria invaded French controlled Bavaria, and requested Prussian military assistance in this attempt to wrest control of Europe from the oppressive Napoleonic regime. This attempt, which might well have succeeded, failed mainly through Friedrich Wilhelm's obsessive fear of French retaliation. The spectre of earlier humiliations haunted the King. Despite a popular desire for action from both the military and civilian population, the King did nothing.

As the French turned on the luckless Austrians, fresh pleas for help arrived. Blücher and the other Generals were anxious to do battle with the hated enemy, but Friedrich Wilhelm, as ever, was too frightened to agree to offer help. He would only offer to help against the French if he received cast iron guarantees of assistance from the Russians.

The King's cowardly behaviour drove dozens of experienced Army officers, incensed at his desertion of his Austrian comrades, to resign their

Karl Friedrich Schinkel, the noted German architect responsible for much of Berlin's finest structures, was also the designer of Germany's most famous military decoration. The design he submitted was preferred to that of the Kaiser himself.

Kaiser Friedrich Wilhelm's projected design for the Iron Cross, eventually rejected in favour of Schinkel's model.

commissions. There was even talk of raising a volunteer legion to fight for Austria without Royal approval.

Inevitably, Austria was defeated, and French pressure on Prussia increased. When Queen Louise died in 1810, one of the few positive voices around the King was lost and Prussia began a decline which ended in 1812 with the final humiliation — Prussia was forced to send almost half her armies to serve under the control of Napoleon's *Grand Armée* in the Russian Campaign.

Following Napoleon's invasion of Russia in June 1812, the Russian forces retreated deep into the country, unintentionally giving Napoleon a false sense of superiority. A new Russian commander, Kutuzov, realised the value of this strategy and led the French even deeper into the vast Russian landscape until, in September, he turned and met them at the fateful battle of Borodino. Although Kutuzov lost 40,000 men to Napoleon's 28,000 Kutuzov was on home ground and could more easily replace his losses from forces held in reserve. Napoleon, on the other hand, had to bring his reserves right across Europe, through nations which were less than friendly to him.

In Prussia particularly, the Generals were well aware of the weakened state of Napoleon's forces as his much vaunted 450,000 strong army was slowly decimated by the Russian armies and by the horrors of the Russian winter. On 29 December 1812, Graf Hans David Ludwig Yorck, leader of the Prussian contingent of Napoleon's *Grand Armée*, withdrew his troops from French command and declared himself neutral. He had in fact already decided that he would come to the aid of Russian troops in his area if they came under French attack.

Even now, Friedrich Wilhelm hesitated to move against the French, fearful of retribution from the many thousands of French troops still garrisoned on Prussian soil. Eventually, with assurances of support from his cousin Czar Alexander, Kaiser Friedrich Wilhelm was finally persuaded of the wisdom and strategic sense of hitting Napoleon at that moment, when he was at his most vulnerable. On 26 February 1813, he signed a defensive and offensive pact with the Czar.

Chancellor Karl von Hardenburg had now managed to persuade the King that a French plot existed against the person of His Majesty himself. Whether this was true or not, it had the desired effect at long last. Friedrich Wilhelm withdrew from the capital, Berlin, and fled to Breslau where, on 13 March 1813, he declared war on France.

The Freedom War had come at last, and with it was created one of the most famous military decorations the world has ever known, the Iron Cross, whose establishment was published in the Prussian newspapers on 20 March 1813. It was always intended to be a temporary award, awarded only during times of war, and would theoretically replace other state awards, the Order of the Red Eagle and the *Pour le Mérite,* during this period.

The process of designing and producing the Iron Cross was very closely followed by its instigator, Friedrich Wilhelm III, who took a very lively interest in the award, submitting his own design proposals. Friedrich Wilhelm's design consisted of a traditional Cross Patte bearing the Royal Cypher in the centre and a spray of oakleaves on each arm. The arms were connected at their roots by a web, and each web carried a single numeral from the date 1813. Some copies of this type of cross are known, but this design was never in fact put into production.

At the same time as the King was working on his design, the noted architect Karl Friedrich Schinkel, designer of many of Berlin's magnificent buildings, was preparing his own sketches and his beautifully simple yet striking design of a simple iron cross shape framed in silver was accepted by the Orders Commission with the King's approval. Production was ordered immediately.

The Iron Cross of 1813 was instituted in three grades: the Grand Cross (Grosskreuz), for award to senior commanders whose leadership was a prime factor in a successful defensive or offensive action, and the Second Class (2 Klasse) and First Class (1 Klasse), to recognise individual gallantry or merit in action.

The Iron Cross Second Class of 1813

The Iron Cross Second Class of 1813 consists of a plain unblackened iron centre, held in a silver frame. The obverse face is devoid of any ornamentation whilst the reverse features a sprig of oakleaves in the centre with the date 1813 on the lower arm, and the Royal Cypher 'FW' and a crown in the upper arm. The award is suspended by means of a ribbon ring attached through an eye welded to the edge of the frame on the upper arm. Through this ring passes a ribbon in the Prussian colours of black and white.

At this early stage in the history of the Iron Cross a great deal of difficulty was experienced in the manufacturing process, especially with welding together of the silver frames. This explains why many of the surviving examples of this award appear to be of rather poor quality and condition. For the same reasons, a number of variants exist, differing particularly in overall size which may range from 28 to 42mm.

A further variation is known where, in place of a ribbon ring, the top arm of the award features three small loops by means of which the award is sewn directly to the ribbon.

Obverse of the 1813 Iron Cross Second Class. The iron centre is plain unblackened metal.

Reverse of the 1813 Iron Cross Second Class. Authorisation was eventually given for this side to be worn as the obverse.

The variation suspension design for the 1813 Second Class. The Cross was sewn directly to the ribbon.

The Iron Cross Banner Top. Established in June 1814 to recognise units which had seen action, it was initially a plain Cross but the Oakleaves were added in September 1814.

It may seem strange that this award would be worn with the blank face as the obverse, and indeed it did become common practice for the award to be worn with the face bearing the oakleaves outwards. This logical idea became so widespread and popular that, in April 1838 the practice was given official sanction and regulations were amended to accommodate this change.

It is generally accepted that the first award of the Iron Cross Second Class was made to Generalleutnant von Borke on 2 April 1813 for the Battle of Luneberg.

Around 16,000 1813 Second Class Iron Crosses were awarded. The exact number is disputed, a number of sources giving various estimates, but, as the original records are now lost, the true figure will probably never be known. It is also known that a handful of 1813 Second Class Crosses were given to female recipients.

The Iron Cross Second Class was awarded to combatant personnel with a ribbon which was principally black, with two white edge stripes. In order to recognise merit or bravery by non-combatant personnel (ie medical orderlies, surgeons, etc) a special ribbon with the colours reversed, a white ribbon with black edge stripes, was produced. The first non-combatant Iron Cross Second Class was awarded to General von Esloeg, military governor of Berlin.

In order to enhance further the esteem in which the winners of the Iron Cross were held, Friedrich Wilhelm ordered that Princes of Royal Blood should only be awarded the Second Class, and on 5 May 1814 the King further ordered, in an amendment to the original statutes, that . . .

Every soldier who died in the performance of an heroic act which, in accordance to the unanimous judgement of his leaders and comrades, would have earned the Iron Cross, shall be honoured after his death by a monument in his Regiment's church at the cost of the State.

The Iron Cross First Class of 1813

More extreme variations of the 1813 First Class are known than of any other Iron Cross, with at least four major types being produced, as follows.

The Ribbon Cross This was produced because of wartime shortages of material, and the difficulty experienced in fabricating the metal version. The Ribbon Cross consists of two pieces of combatant Iron Cross ribbon crossed at right angles in the approximate shape of the Iron Cross. This Ribbon Cross was sewn directly on to the tunic.

The Fabric Cross This variant consists of a piece of cardboard in the shape of the Iron Cross, which is covered in black velvet. The outline to this is edged in silver wire. Once again this type of award was intended to be sewn directly to the tunic.

The so-called 'Bandkreuz' ribbon version of the Iron Cross First Class was a short-lived forerunner of the Iron Cross proper.

Below
Two variant versions of the 1813 First Class. The example on the left has a velvet centre.

Bottom
Reverse of 1813 First Class Crosses showing the typical loops for attachment to the tunic.

The wide-rimmed version of the 1813 Iron Cross First Class.

The Standard Cross This was the formal official version. It consists of a plain blank iron cross without design, and framed with silver. The reverse face is a plain silver blank onto which are welded eight small loops, two in each arm. These loops allow the award to be sewn directly to the tunic. The overall size of the award is around 40mm but, although this overall size is fairly consistent, the width of the silver rim may be found to vary considerably depending on the maker.

The Composite Cross This type is a combination of the last two described, being basically a metal Iron Cross but with a black velvet centre. It may well have been an unofficial alteration to an existing piece, but is certainly contemporary.

It is said that pinback Iron Crosses were also made, in the same style as First Classes from later years. It may be that these are official replacement awards for Iron Crosses which had been lost, and that they were made in later years when assembly techniques had improved enough to allow easy manufacture of such types.

The total number of First Class awards was around 635 to 670, the first being awarded to General von Helwig on 17 April 1813 at the Battle of Warfed. The 1813 Iron Cross First and Second Class awards are broken down as follows by A E Prowse in his book *The Iron Cross of Prussia and Germany.*

	OFFICERS		LOWER RANKS		POSTHUMOUS	
Class	*First*	*Second*	*First*	*Second*	*First*	*Second*
Unassigned	143	264	-	11	-	-
Infantry	233	1276	48	3073	256	3296
Reserve Infantry	35	652	2	1029	370	994
Cavalry	97	517	15	894	100	1071
Reserve Cavalry	12	186	-	342	78	297
Artillery	43	192	2	529	33	394
Engineers	5	62	-	1	7	32
Adminstration	-	3	-	1	-	-
Totals	568	3152	67	5880	844	6084

A rare example of the Russian-made Kulm Cross

THE KULM CROSS

Instituted by Friedrich Wilhelm III on 4 December 1813, the Kulm Cross was intended to honour the bravery of Russian Guards units commanded by Count Ostermann-Tolstoy, against the French under General Vandamme, at Kulm. The allied armies had been in retreat after a disastrous defeat at Dresden in mid August, and the gallantry of the Russian troops under Ostermann-Tolstoy was instrumental in the defeat of the pursuing French at Kulm, holding the French at bay until Kleist arrived, at a great cost in casualties. The King decided to reward the bravery of the Russians by awarding them a special version of the Iron Cross, although, for some unknown reason, three years was to elapse before the official awards were made.

The following extract was published in a Russian magazine in August 1816 . . .

On the twenty fourth day of this month, badges of the Iron Cross were received here. His Majesty the King of Prussia has royally condescended to assignate these for award to members of the Guards units who, with exceptional courage fought at Kulm on the seventeenth day of August 1813.

The number of awards sent, 11,563, was related to the number of troops who were involved in the battle. In fact, only 7131 survived to take part in the presentation ceremony. Over 4400 had died in battle or had subsequently perished as a result of their wounds.

In fact, on hearing of the awards, many Guardsmen had produced their own awards by attaching black leather crosses onto metal backing cut from belt buckles. The awards officially presented were factory made in Prussia in lacquered silver for officers, and iron for other ranks. Although factory made, they were inferior in quality to the Prussian Iron Crosses.

The total intended number of awards was as follows: generals, nine; staff officers, forty-four; officers, 371; NCO's, 1168; corporals, 404; other ranks, 10,070.

The Grand Cross of the Iron Cross of 1813

The 1813 Grand Cross consists of a large unpainted cast iron centre set in a silver rim. As with the Second Class, the obverse is absolutely plain, and the reverse is decorated with a spray of oakleaves in the centre, the date 1813 on the lower and the 'FW' cypher and crown on the upper arm. The only difference to the Second Class reverse is the use of four acorns on the oak stem instead of two. Suspension is by means of a vertical silver loop through which passed a 57mm wide neck ribbon. The ribbon is in the same colours as that of the Second Class.

The Grand Cross was made in three pieces, the iron centre and a two part silver frame. Its overall size is 64mm. The quality of manufacture is much finer than that of the First and Second Classes.

The Grand Cross was awarded only seven times. It should be noted that original examples of the Grand Cross are of the highest rarity. Many of the apparently original pieces encountered today may be copies made in the late nineteenth century or later for museum displays, etc.

THE 1813 GRAND CROSS RECIPIENTS

Generalfeldmarschall Gebhard Leberecht Fürst Blücher von Wahlstatt Probably the most famous of all the 1813 Grand Cross recipients, Blücher was awarded the decoration on 26 August 1813, in recognition of his leadership during the battle of Katzbach.

Blücher's aggressive spirit was frustrated by his orders not to engage the enemy in a full scale battle, but to play 'cat and mouse' with the French and wear down their troops until such time as the Prussians were ready to attack.

This opportunity came when the French troops, commanded by Jaques MacDonald, Duke of Taranto, crossed the River Katzbach. The French marched straight into the arms of the waiting Prussian and Russian troops. MacDonald had around 50,000 troops to face Blücher's 80,000. The weary and demoralised French troops were no match for the allies and in the fearful battle which ensued they were cut to pieces by artillery fire and infantry and cavalry attacks.

MacDonald left half his force on the battlefield dead or wounded. Many of his men were drowned in the waters of the Katzbach. Blücher lost just over 3000 men.

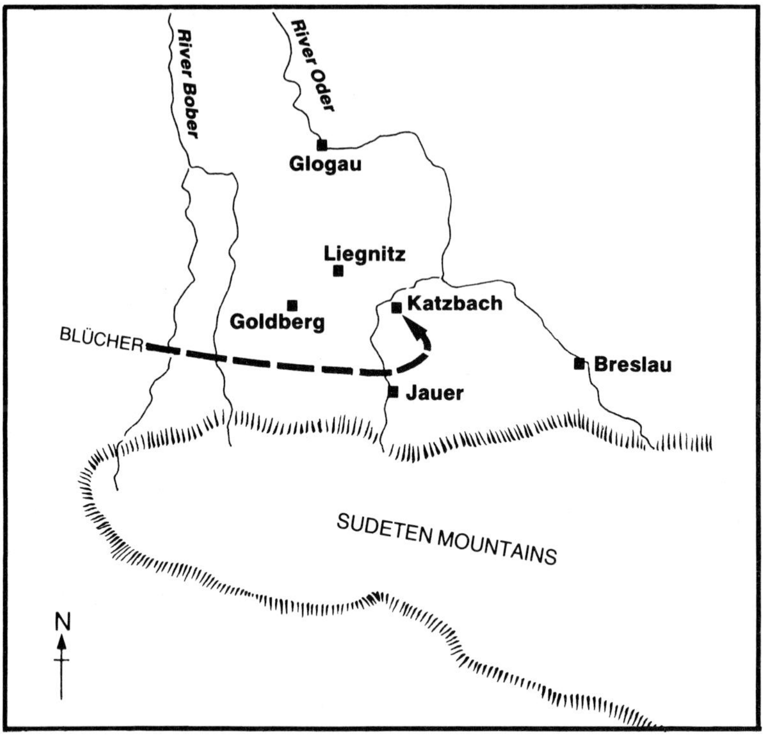

Blücher's retreat to Katzbach, scene of his great victory.

Blücher's Grand Cross was a fitting reward for his magnificent victory over a powerful enemy, atrocious weather and the rumblings of discontent in his own forces.

Blücher was further honoured on 3 June 1814 by the award of the title *Fürst* (Prince) Blücher von Wahlstatt, an honour which he accepted only with reluctance. Blücher indeed took much greater pleasure in the title awarded to him by his adoring troops — 'Papa Blücher'.

General Friedrich Kleist von Nollendorf and Generalleutnant Ostermann-Tolstoy These two awards were made on 29 August 1813 in recognition of the part played by these officers in the victory at Kulm. Doubt exists, however, as to whether the decorations were ever presented, and they may have been made on paper only.

Falling back towards Toplitz before the advancing forces of General Vandamme, the allies, under the Austrian Prince Eugen, suddenly counter

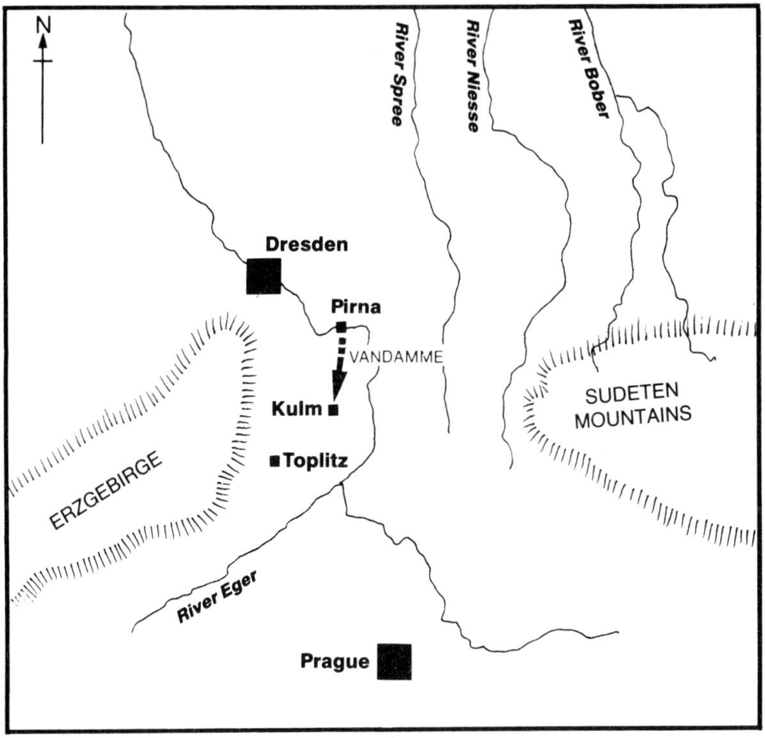

The area around Kulm, south of Dresden, where Vandamme met his defeat.

attacked. Under the cover of this attack, reinforcements under the command of the Russian Generalleutnant Ostermann-Tolstoy were brought on to the field of battle between Vandamme and the town of Toplitz. In the furious fighting which developed, the Russians fought with great gallantry, Ostermann-Tolstoy himself losing an arm.

At this point, with Ostermann-Tolstoy to their front and the Austrians under Prince Eugen on their flank, the French were dismayed to find fresh Prussian troops under Kleist coming up at the rear, and were forced to turn and meet him. Now under attack from three sides, Vandamme's position was becoming desperate. Trapped in this mountainous region with no avenue of escape open to him and having suffered heavy losses, Vandamme surrendered.

A total of 10,000 of his men were killed or wounded and a further 7000 were taken prisoner by the victorious allied forces.

General der Infanterie Friedrich Wilhelm Graf Bülow von Dennewitz Born on 16 February 1775, Bülow was one of Blücher's ablest officers. His skilful surprise attack on Napoleon's favourite, Marshal Ney, at Dennewitz just 55 kilometres south west of Berlin, resulted in a French defeat with 9000 killed or wounded and 15,000 taken prisoner. Coming hard on the heels of his victory over Marshal Gerard at Hagelberg, this morale boosting victory brought Bülow the award of the Grand Cross on 6 September 1813. He was also honoured with the title *Graf* (Count) in recognition of his victory.

Crown Prince Carl Johann (Bernadotte) of Sweden The son of a Frenchman, Carl Johann was born in 1763 and saw his first military service in the Italian Army in 1780. He married the sister-in-law of Napoleon's brother and this family connection brought him command of I Corps of the *Grand Armée*. Napoleon did not much like this relative and found his military prowess equally unimpressive. It was in fact only his family connection which prevented his Court Martial after his poor performance at the Battle of Jena.

His favourable treatment of Swedish prisoners however, stood him in good stead with that country and, after Napoleon sacked him for his disastrous performance at the battle of Wagram in 1809, the Swedes came forward and elected him Crown Prince. Drawn into conflict again with Napoleon when the French entered Swedish Pomerania in 1812, Carl Johann allied himself first with the Russians and ultimately with Prussia. Carl Johann was never a brilliant field commander and it is thought by some that his award of the Grand Cross was made more for political and diplomatic reasons.

Carl Johann ultimately became King Charles XIV of Sweden. Papers in the Swedish National Archives show that his Grand Cross was returned to Prussia after his death.

General Hans David Ludwig von Yorck Yorck's Grand Cross was awarded in recognition of his bravery and leadership from the Battle of Laon through to the surrender of Paris. The exact date of the award is not known, but it was made sometime during 1814.

After a disastrous defeat south west of Laon, Blücher's forces had retreated behind the town's defences, pursued by Napoleon. Laon, however, occupied a good natural defensive position on a hill site giving a fine command of the surrounding plain, and had been much reinforced.

General Graf Bülow von Dennewitz. The extreme size of the Grand Cross compared with the other decorations worn at the neck is noteworthy.

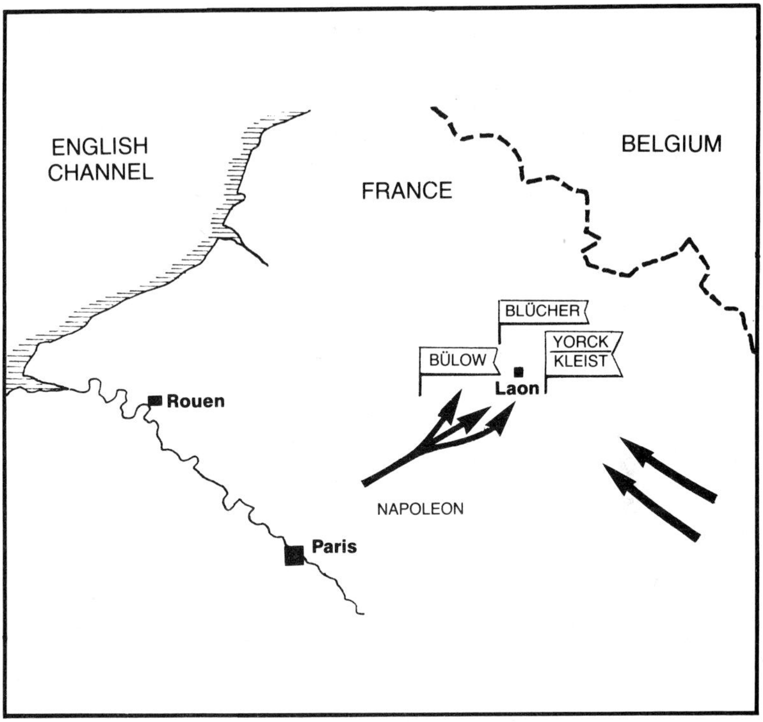

Napoleon's fateful attack on the Prussian forces at Laon.

Opposite
Crown Prince Carl Johann of Sweden. As well as the Grand Cross worn at the neck, the First Class can be seen on the left breast.

General Graf Yorck von Wartenburg, one of the heroes of the Battle of Laon.

Napoleon gravely misjudged the position and underestimated Blücher's remaining strength. His attacks on Laon were little short of suicidal and after some slight initial advances, his forces were routed.

As the weary French troops rested round their camp fires for the night, Yorck's battle hardened infantry and cavalry surrounded them and fell upon them. The panic stricken French were put to flight.

With the glittering prize of Paris within his grasp, Blücher fell ill and squabbling broke out amongst his officers. Gneisenau, his chief of staff, took command and reversed Blücher's orders for the pursuit of the French. A furious Yorck resigned his command and set off on his way home to Prussia. Only a personal plea from Blücher himself persuaded him to return, and indeed Yorck's leadership during the next three weeks leading to the fall of Paris on 31 March 1814 was an essential ingredient of the allied victory. Yorck, like Blücher, was also rewarded with a title, *Count* Yorck von Wartenburg in honour of an earlier victory at Wartenburg in October 1813.

Friedrich Bogislaw Emanuel Graf Tauentzein von Wittenberg
Born in Potsdam on 26 September 1760, Tauentzein attended the Military College in Berlin and started his career as a Standartenoberjunker in Regiment Gens d'Armes (Nr 10). Becoming an ensign in Infanterie Regiment Nr 35 'Prinz Heinrich', he progressed well, reaching the rank of Major by the age of thirty. His varied experience included service as liaison officer with the Austrians in the Netherlands during 1792.

By 1813, Tauentzein had attained the rank of Generalleutnant and was military governor of the area between the Oder and Weichsel. In the Freedom War, his forces took part in the Battle of Dennewitz and the occupation of Wittenberg (Tauentzein gaining the Iron Cross Second and First Classes) as well as the siege of Magdeburg.

Amongst the decorations which recognised Tauentzein's military prowess were the Russian Order of George III, which he was given Prussian Royal Sanction to wear, and the Knights Cross of the Order of the Black Eagle awarded for his part in the Battle of Jüterbog.

On 8 December, Tauentzein was promoted to full General and this honour was followed on 26 January 1814 by the award of the Grand Cross. This award was for continued success rather than for one specific action.

As with a number of his contemporaries, Tauentzein was awarded a title in recognition of his successes. On 3 June 1814 he became *Graf* Tauentzein von Wittenberg.

Tauentzein's career, however, was not without controversy. He had clashed with Gneisenau and became involved in a dispute with Bülow over the credit for the victory at Wittenberg. It took the personal intervention of

General Graf Tauentzein von Wittenberg.

the King to resolve this dispute, in favour of Bülow. Tauentzein, however, was somewhat placated with the award of an estate at Schönefeld in Züllichau-Schweibus, a former Monastery.

Amongst Tauentzein's other appointments were Commanding General of IV Army Corps (1815), Commanding General of III Army Corps (1820), and Colonel in Chief of 20 Infanterie Regiment, which bore his name as an honour title until 1918.

Friedrich Bogislaw Emanuel Graf Tauentzein von Wittenberg died in Berlin on 20 February 1824 at the age of sixty-three. He was buried in Berlin's Invalidenkirchhof.

THE STAR TO THE GRAND CROSS

This special award was presented only once, to Generalfeldmarschall Blücher in recognition of his part in the defeat of Napoleon at Waterloo (or the Battle of La Belle Alliance as it was known to the Prussians). Hence, it is the 'Blücherstern'. The story of the Battle of Waterloo has been too well covered in countless other books to warrant re-telling here. Suffice it to say that the timely arrival of Blücher and his Prussians may well have

Opposite
Generalfeldmarschall Blucher, the sole recipient of the 1813 Star to the Grand Cross, shown here wearing this award together with the Grand Cross itself.

The 'Blücherstern', Star to the Grand Cross of the Iron Cross of 1813

prevented the battle going either way. Although somewhat unwilling to give a foreign commander credit for his great victory, even the Duke of Wellington admitted that Blücher 'deserved full credit for preventing a British defeat'.

A popular figure in Britain, Blücher had received a rapturous welcome when he visited the United Kingdom after the fall of Paris in 1814. Indeed, he was so moved by his welcome that he swore he would never leave Britain had he not had a family at home in Prussia.

His own people were even more devoted to him and, having awarded him the Grand Cross for the Battle of Katzbach, an entirely new decoration was crafted for him after the Battle of Waterloo. On 26 June 1815, he was awarded the Star to the Grand Cross. This decoration consisted of a hand crafted, solid gold, eight-pointed radiant star upon which was superimposed a small Iron Cross in the centre. It is thought to have measured around 77mm overall, and the Iron Cross 33mm. The original Star was destroyed by fire in 1820, however, so the exact details remain somewhat speculative.

As well as the award of the Star, Blücher was given the honour of having the Iron Cross incorporated into his personal coat of arms, an honour extended to only one other person, Prussian chancellor Karl von Hardenburg.

THE IRON CROSS OF 1870

Under the formidable statesmanship of Otto von Bismarck, Prussia had expanded in both economic and military terms at an incredible rate and, apart from a brief and unsuccessful outbreak of revolutionary activity during 1848, experienced a period of peace and prosperity until 1864. Then, a dispute with Denmark over the territories of Schleswig-Holstein led to a combined Austro-Prusso-Bavarian invasion of these parts. The Danes were quickly subdued. This tripartite alliance, however, was short lived, and in 1866 Prussia took over sole control of Schleswig-Holstein.

Within a few weeks, Prussia had also taken control of Saxony, Hannover and Hesse and had defeated the Austrians at the Battle of Königgratz, leaving itself as the undisputed master of most of Germany, with the exception of the Catholic south. Prussia did, however, have secret treaties with most of these states, and also with Russia in the east, and could thus feel secure.

The astute statesmanship of Bismarck led to Austria being given a very favourable peace settlement. No occupation troops were to be stationed on Austrian soil, nor were crippling reparations to be sought. Bismarck knew that the French were the greatest potential enemy to Prussia's aspirations, and he wanted friendly relations with the Austrians in case of any future European conflict.

France, no doubt expecting the support of the Catholic southern German states in any conflict, also felt secure. They were to be proved disastrously wrong.

With the neighbouring states aligned on the side of Prussia, Spain was the only real potential ally for France against Prussia, but even this loophole was sealed when a German Hohenzollern Prince was offered the Spanish throne.

The French emperor, Napoleon III, was understandably furious at the thought of his southern neighbour coming under Prussian influence. Unaware of the real strength of the rising tide of German nationalism that was sweeping through the individual German states, Napoleon traded insults freely with the Prussians in the exchange of diplomatic letters which followed. These were skilfully engineered by Bismarck to provoke the French into declaring was on Prussia in July of 1870. The French

A typical 1870 Group, comprising Iron Cross Second Class, Franco-Prussian War Medal for Combatants, and Kaiser Wilhelm I Commemorative Medal.

The German advances across France in the brief Franco-Prussian War.

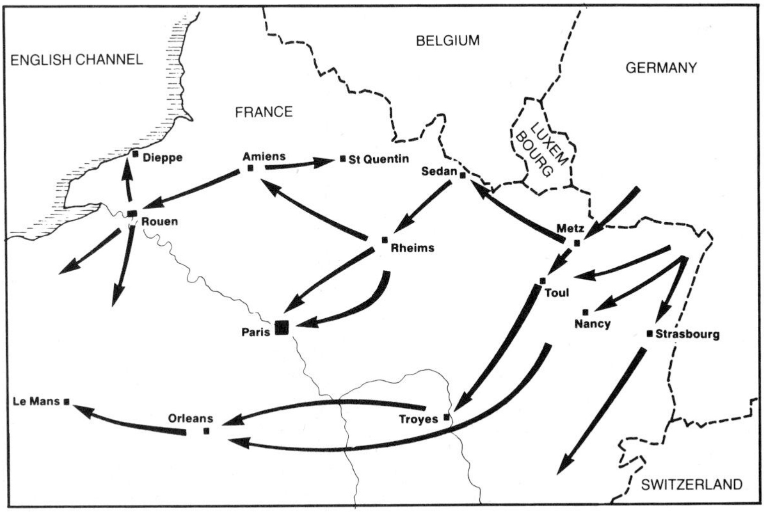

confidently expected the south German states to align themselves with France, and were horrified when the Germans stood solidly behind Prussia.

The German forces swept into France and within four short weeks the French army was surrounded in Metz and the Emperor, on his way to the front, was captured by the Prussians at Sedan. The French army had been destroyed.

The French government in Paris, however, was still intact, and reserve forces were quickly mobilised to meet the Prussians. Partisans in the Prussian rear were also beginning to take their toll, despite savage Prussian reprisals.

The French had more to think about than the Prussians, however, as revolutionary fervour swept through Paris and the *communards* erected barricades in the streets. The French were horrified that this hotbed of Marxism should erupt in their capital city, and the Prussians were equally anxious about any possible sympathy which might arise for the *communards* in their own country. In order to circumvent this, the Prussians and the French government came to terms. The French forces would attack the commune, whilst Prussian units supported them with artillery bombardment of the commune area. On 28 May, two months after it was declared, and after a short but gallant resistance, the commune surrendered. Prussia was victorious and German nationalism reached its peak when, on 18 June 1871, the Prussian King was declared Emperor of all Germany.

The Franco-Prussian War had seen not only the humiliating defeat of the powerful French army in just a few short months, but the unification of the German states into one of the world's great powers. Fittingly, King Wilhelm I of Prussia had issued a proclamation on 19 July 1870 which once again instituted the Iron Cross. This proclamation read as follows:

. . . We, Wilhelm, by the grace of God, King of Prussia, considering the grave situation of the fatherland, and in grateful memory of our forefathers heroic deeds during the great years of the wars of independence wish to revive the concept of the Iron Cross donated by my father who is resting with God. The Iron Cross has to be conferred without making any class or position distinctions, as a commendation of a distinguished service earned in combat with the enemy, or at home, in view of this struggle to preserve the honour and independence of our dear fatherland.

Consequently we order as follows:

1. The Iron Cross Order which has been recalled into existence during this war has to consist, as in former times, of two classes and one Grand Cross. The decoration, as well as the ribbon, does not change, but on the front the letter 'W' with Crown, and the date 1870, are to be affixed.
2. The second class will be hung from a black ribbon with white trim if the distinguished service has been earned in combat with the enemy, and on a white

ribbon with black trim if this is not the case, and worn in the buttonhole, whereas the first class is to be worn on the left breast, and the Grand Cross, twice the size of the other two classes, will be worn from a cravat around the neck.
3. The second class is to be conferred first; the first class can only be conferred if the second class has already been earned. The first class is to be worn beside the second class cross.
4. The Grand Cross can be earned by the Commandant of a garrison exclusively, either for a victorious combat after which the enemy has to leave its position, or for capturing an important fortress, or for a persistent defence of a fortress which finally did not fall into the enemy's hands.
5. All advantages which have been in connection with the possession of the first and second class Military Honour Medal pass over to the first and second class Iron Cross, with the proviso of a constitutional regulation of a promise to honour.

Attested with our own handwriting, signature and royal seal, Berlin, 19 July 1870.

WILHELM

Signed,

Bismarch-Schoenhausen von Roon
Eulenberg Leonhardt von Camphausen
Itzenplitz von Geschow

The Iron Cross Second Class of 1870

The 1870 second class measures 42mm, and features the same reverse design as its 1813 predecessor. The obverse features the date 1870 on the

The Iron Cross Second Class of 1870. This example has the Non-Combatant ribbon.

lower arm, the letter 'W' in the centre, and the crown in the upper arm. As with the 1813 type, the 1870 second class is suspended via a ribbon ring attached to the upper arm. No regulations were laid down for the ribbon width which may range from 10 to 26mm.

Due partly to the fact that a number of 1870 Iron Crosses were made *after* the close of the war, but for actions during the war, estimates of the number of awards made are rather confused. By averaging out various estimates we can arrive at a figure of around 41,770 awards of which approximately 3500 were non-combatant.

A number of British recipients of the 1870 Iron Cross are known, generally as non-combatant decorations, and include General Sir C P B Walker, Surgeon-General J H K Innes, General Sir Henry Brakenbury, GCB, Surgeon-General W G N Manley, VC, CB, and Captain Sir James Lumsden Seaton.

General Manley, VC is a particularly interesting case. In charge of B Division of the British Ambulance, attached to the Prussian 22 Infanterie Division, Manley received the Iron Cross for his 'devoted and excellent conduct in seeking and caring for the wounded of the 22 Division in the actions of Chateauneuf and Bretoncelle on 18 and 21 November, and the

Opposite
Combatant and Non-Combatant versions of the Iron Cross Second Class of 1870 with the Twenty-Fifth Anniversary Oakleaves.

Right
The Iron Cross First Class of 1870.

battles of Orleans and Cravant on 10 December 1870'. This award was made to Manley at the personal request of the Prussian Crown Prince. Manley later saw action at the seige of Paris and was decorated by the French for his care of their wounded.

The Iron Cross First Class of 1870

The 1870 first class is a much more finely executed decoration than its 1813 counterpart. Size was fairly standardised and most pieces that are encountered measure around 41mm, but a few may be encountered which are a millimetre or two larger. The obverse has the same design as the second class. The reverse has a hinged vertical pin fitting, and often two hooks on the horizontal arms. These helped to secure the cross on the wearer's tunic.

Special 'Prinzen' sizes are also encountered. These are often considerably smaller than the normal size and may be finely executed in silver and enamel. These crosses were so named because of their popularity with members of the German Royal Families.

The total number of 1870 first class awards ranges from 1230 to 1903 depending upon which reference source is consulted, but most sources seem to agree at a figure somewhere around 1300. The first award of an 1870 first class went to Generalfeldmarschall von Steinmek, a veteran of the Freedom Wars who had already won the second class Iron Cross of 1813.

THE TWENTY-FIFTH ANNIVERSARY OAKLEAVES

On the twenty-fifth anniversary of the Franco-Prussian War, in 1895, Kaiser Wilhelm I instituted a special set of oakleaves to commemorate the recipients who had won the Iron Cross of 1870. The award consists of a spray of three oakleaves, measuring 26 by 18mm with the number '25' in the centre. These oakleaves were worn on the ribbon of the Iron Cross second class, just above the ribbon ring. Some variants are known, as are miniatures on buttonhole mountings for wear on the lapel of civilian jackets.

A buttonhole version of the Twenty-Fifth Anniversary Oakleaves for wear with civilian clothes.

Opposite
Crown Prince Friedrich Wilhelm of Prussia. The Feldmarschall rank insignia on the shoulder strap and the details of the Grand Cross and *Pour le Mérite* are clearly visible in this fine portrait. Note how far down the chest the Grand Cross is worn.

The Grand Cross of the Iron Cross of 1870

The Grand Cross of 1870 differs very little from the 1813 type, being a 64–65mm silver framed iron Cross Patte. It retains the reverse design of the 1813 piece, but has the new obverse as featured on the 1870 first and second classes.

The 1870 Grand Cross has a similar style eyelet and ribbon loop to that on its predecessor. However, whereas the 1813 Grand Cross usually had a plain unblackened iron centre, the 1870 Grand Cross centre *was* normally blackened.

The 1870 Grand Cross ribbon is in the same colours as the 1813 piece but wider at 67mm rather than 57mm.

A total of only eight 1870 Grand Crosses were awarded, excluding the Grand Cross which the Kaiser himself wore at the request of his Generals from 16 June 1871. Considering the relatively short time span of the Franco-Prussian war, the number of Grand Crosses awarded was rather high. From the declaration of war on 19 July 1870 to the final surrender of the French and the convention of Versailles in January 1871, only a few

Obverse of the Grand Cross of the Iron Cross of 1870. Note the very small eye for the ribbon loop, and the narrow silver rim.

General von Göben. This study dates from before the award of the Grand Cross.

Generalfeldmarschall von Manteuffel. The Grand Cross is worn above the *Pour le Mérite.*

months had passed, although, in fact, there were no real set piece battles after the French surrender at Sedan and Napoleon's capture. The remaining period of the war was taken up mainly with the siege of Paris and occupation duties.

However, although Generalfeldmarschall Kronprinz Friedrich Wilhelm of Prussia was awarded the Grand Cross on 22 March 1871 to recognise actions at Weisenburg and Wörth the previous year, and General der Infanterie von Werder was awarded the Grand Cross in 1871 in recognition of his successful battle at Strasburg in 1870, most of the 1870 Grand Crosses were awarded to recognise a period of meritorious service rather than a specific action as the original statutes intended. The other six Grand Crosses were awarded to General der Infanterie von Göben and General der Kavellerie Freiherr von Manteuffel, in 1871, for their duties as commander-in-chief of the First Army during the war, and commander of the Southern Army, respectively, and, on 22 March 1871, to three other Generalfeldmarschalls, Helmuth von Möltke, Kronprinz Albert Friedrich Augustus, and Prinz Friedrich Karl Nicolaus, to recognise their services as chief of staff, commander of the Maas Army, and commander of the Second Army, respectively, while the sixth was awarded to General Grossherzog von Mecklenburg-Schwerin on 16 June 1871 for his services as commander of the Loire Army.

General von Werder. The artist has shown the Grand Cross with its reverse face outwards.

Generalfeldmarschall Graf Möltke. The Grand Cross is shown to good effect against the plain dark uniform.

Crown Prince Albert Friedrich Augustus of Saxony. Once again the Grand Cross is worn above the *Pour le Mérite.*

Grand Duke Friedrich Franz of Mecklenburg-Schwerin. Here, the Grand Cross is worn below the *Pour le Mérite.*

Kaiser Wilhelm I. Note how far down the chest the Grand Cross is worn. The award at the neck is the *Pour le Mérite.*

Prince Friedrich Karl of Prussia. The Second Class Iron Cross is of the small 'Prinzen' variety.

THE IRON CROSS OF 1914

The declaration of King Wilhelm I of Prussia as the Emperor of all Germany at the Palace of Versailles in June 1871 saw the culmination of Bismarck's ambitions for the unification of Germany. Henceforth any potential enemy would face, not a motley collection of disorganised states, but one of the most powerful countries in Europe. For the next seventeen years, Bismarck continued to serve his country well, with his customary diplomatic skill.

In 1888, however, Kaiser Wilhelm I died, and within a few months he had been succeeded by Wilhelm II. Bismarck and Wilhelm II despised each other with equal strength of feeling, and Bismarck retired shortly afterwards, dying in 1889.

In the twenty-five years following Bismarck's death, Wilhelm II's lust for power, untempered by Bismarck's caution and statesmanship, was to lose Germany most of her friends. Those who had been neutral became distrusting and suspicious of Wilhelm's intentions. Despite the diplomatic decline, Germany continued to grow in strength both militarily and economically, with a powerful army and fleet which, though inferior in numbers to the Royal Navy of Great Britain, was nevertheless newer and better gunned.

Wilhelm's support of the Boer forces in the Transvaal was construed by Britain as very hostile, and his ambition in building up the German fleet was seen as a very dangerous move. To counter Germany's military build up, Britain moved closer to an alliance with her old enemy, France, and thereby with Russia. Germany was becoming isolated in Europe, a fate which Bismarck had so long and successfully avoided.

The direct causes of World War One, culminating in the assassination of Archduke Ferdinand in Sarajevo, are too well documented in countless history books to warrant repetition here. With the coming of the World War, the Iron Cross was again instituted, on 5 August 1914.

It is interesting to note that the Iron Cross was not awarded to German troops for action during the Boxer Rebellion in China, or for action in South West Africa, but when the whole nation was mobilised for a major conflict, Germany's premier military decoration was once again instituted. The institution statement read as follows:

A typical 1914 Iron Cross grouping comprising, Iron Cross Second Class, Cross of Honour with Swords, Baltic Cross, and First War Service Medal.

An unidentified group of recently decorated Army officers. Note the variety of methods by which the Crosses are attached to the buttonholes.

. . . We, Wilhelm, by the grace of God, King of Prussia, etc . . . in view of the serious position in which our beloved fatherland has been put, by being forced into a war, and in thankful remembrance of our forefathers' heroic achievements during the exciting years of the liberation wars and the struggle for Germany's union, we wish to renew again the Iron Cross donated by my Great Grandfather who is resting with God.

The Iron Cross is to be awarded without exception to all persons of the Army, Navy and the Home Guard, the members of the volunteer nursing units and to all other persons who offered their service to the Army or Navy or are designated as Army or Navy officers. The award will be made for every sacrifice made in the war. Further, all persons who earn it, by serving the needs of the German Empire and their allies at home, may receive the cross.

1. The donation of the Iron Cross, which has been renewed for this war, has to consist of two classes and one Grand Cross, as in former times. The decoration, as well as the ribbon, will remain unchanged. On the front will be the 'W' with the crown above, and the year 1914 will be placed in the lower arm.
2. The second class Cross will be worn on a black ribbon with white trim, in the buttonhole, if it has been awarded for combat. For awards at home, this Cross will be worn on a white ribbon with black trim. The first class is worn on the left breast and the Grand Cross at the neck.
3. The first class is only awarded if the second class has already been earned and is worn beside the latter one.
4. The awarding of the Grand Cross does not depend on the previous earning of a first or second class Cross. It can be awarded only for a decisively won battle in which the enemy had to leave his position, or for the independent and successful leadership of an army or navy contingent or for the conquest of a fortress, or for defending an important fortress.

All privileges in connection with the Military Honour Medal First and Second Class with the proviso of the constitutional regulations of the donation, pass over to the Iron Cross first and second class.

Documentary and with our own hand signature and the King's seal.
Berlin, 5 August 1914

WILHELM.

A further statute was published in 1915, being principally an enlargement of the original, to include a clause stating that the Iron Cross could be awarded to individuals of all the central powers.

In June 1915, yet another statute was published. This introduced the 1914 Bar to the 1870 Iron Cross, and was worded as follows:

. . . The owners of the Iron Cross second class of 1870-1871 who have earned during the present war, in combat or at home, the same decoration for special services, will get a special silver clasp or bar which will be attached to the ribbon of the Iron Cross above the silver jubilee oakleaves. The bar bears a miniature of the Iron Cross and the date 1914 . . .

Given at General Headquarters, June 4, 1915.

The Iron Cross Second Class of 1914

The Iron Cross Second Class of 1914 is identical to its 1870 predecessor with only the date in the lower arm altered from 1870 to 1914. The 1914 Iron Cross Second Class pieces are generally found to be of fairly high quality manufacture with the exception of some solid brass one piece castings made in the latter part of the war. The size was standardised at around 42mm, but many smaller 'Prinzen' sizes were also made. Early specimens were manufactured with a genuine silver frame, and the ribbon suspension rings on these pieces are normally found to be marked with the '800' or '900' silver hallmark. Minor variants may be found, with the oakleaf decoration either of convex or concave appearance, and the size of the letter 'W' and the numerals may vary considerably. The ribbon may be found in widths varying from 25 to 30mm.

Estimates of the number of 1914 second class awards vary enormously,

The Iron Cross Second Class of 1914. This example has the Non-Combatant ribbon.

An Iron Cross Second Class of 1914 with an unusual unofficial commemorative bar, '1914-1915'.

Two examples of the 1914 Iron Cross Second Class showing variants of the triangular style ribbon common on awards to Austrian personnel.

A steel helmeted infantry officer attaches a newly awarded Iron Cross Second Class to the buttonhole of the recipient. Note the Pickelhaube worn by the officer on the left.

A recently decorated Leutnant wearing the Iron Cross Second Class at the buttonhole. Note the bandages just showing under his cap.

from around 1.5 million to over 5 million. Even the lower figure would represent a very liberal award policy.

Amongst these numerous awards, there are some fascinating individual cases. In his book on the Iron Cross, A E Prowse quotes the case of the Nigerian soldier Chari Maigumeri. A Regimental Sergeant Major of the Third Battalion, the Nigeria Regiment, he had originally served in the Imperial German Army in the Cameroons and had been decorated with the Iron Cross Second Class for gallantry in action against the British during the West African campaign. Captured by the British, he then served with the British West African Frontier Force and distinguished himself again in action with his new masters.

By 1928, Maigumeri was an RSM with Third Battalion, the Nigerian Regiment. He won the Military Medal during the 1940–1941 campaign in Abyssinia against the Italians, and later, on the Far Eastern Front, he was mentioned in dispatches whilst serving in Burma against the Japanese. In 1944, he was awarded the British Empire Medal for long and loyal service to the Crown.

Of all the many recipients of the 1914 Iron Cross Second Class, few can have had such an interesting career as Chari Maigumeri.

III. bayr. Armee-Korps.

Vorläufiges Besitz-Zeugnis.

Am 30. Dezember 1914 ist

dem

des K. 10. Regiments

im Namen Seiner Majestät des Deutschen Kaisers

Wilhelm II.

König von Preußen

das Eiserne Kreuz 2. Klasse verliehen worden.

Der Kommandierende General:

General der Kavallerie.

A 1914 dated citation for the Iron Cross Second Class to an infantryman in a Bavarian Infantry Regiment.

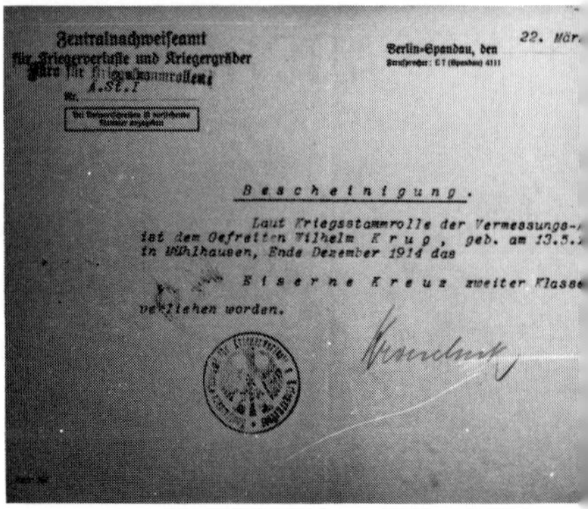

Zentralnachweiseamt für Kriegerverluste und Kriegergräber

Berlin-Spandau, den 22. Mär

Bescheinigung.

Laut Kriegsstammrolle der Vermessungs- ist dem Gefreiten Wilhelm Krug, geb. am in Mühlhausen, Ende Dezember 1914 das Eiserne Kreuz zweiter Klasse verliehen worden.

A post-war (1934) confirmation of the award of the 1914 Iron Cross Second Class to a Gefreiter Wilhelm Krug.

A rather elaborate citation to a soldier in a Westphalian infantry regiment.

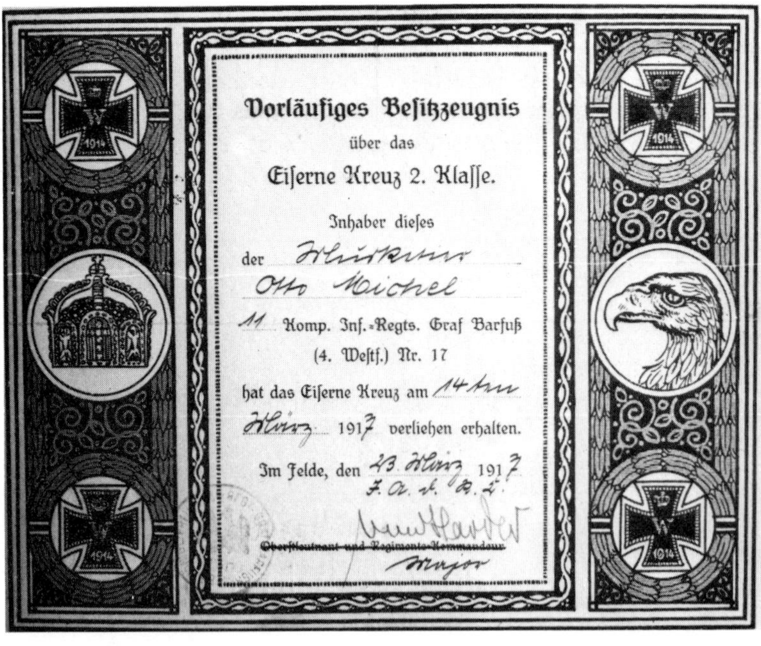

Vorläufiges Besitzzeugnis

über das

Eiserne Kreuz 2. Klasse.

Inhaber dieses

der Musketier

Otto Michel

11 Komp. Inf.-Regts. Graf Barfuß (4. Westf.) Nr. 17

hat das Eiserne Kreuz am 14ten März 1917 verliehen erhalten.

Im Felde, den 23. März 1917

~~Oberstleutnant und Regiments-Kommandeur~~

Major

The Iron Cross First Class of 1914

The Iron Cross First Class of 1914 comprises the usual Cross Patte in black painted or lacquered iron, with a silver frame to the obverse and plain silver reverse. The design of the obverse is identical to that of the Second Class. In the early years at least, the frame was genuine silver and the silver content mark may often be found on the reverse of these pieces. The 1914 Iron Cross First Class normally measures about 41mm. More variants are known of the 1914 Iron Cross First Class than of any other Iron Cross. The number of attachments available ranged from pin fittings, clips, washers, screw, etc, to nuts and bolts.

The type of First Class usually actually awarded, was a flat type with a standard vertical hinged pin fitting on the reverse. During the first two years of the war, this was the type normally encountered. From 1915 onwards however, convexed crosses became very popular and with them all sorts of elaborate fittings, particularly screwbacks, became available to those who wished to purchase additional pieces at their own expense.

Towards the end of World War One, as materials became scarce, the general quality of the Iron Cross deteriorated, with silver plate being used in place of real silver, and various alloys in place of the iron centre. One piece strikings are also known from this period.

The Iron Cross First Class of 1914.

Reverse of a typical Screwback version of the 1914 Iron Cross First Class.

1914 Iron Crosses First Class can also be encountered in a bewildering variety of cases. These may range from simple black boxes to elaborate miniatures of Pickelhaubes Helmets, with the award concealed within, on a fitted velvet base. Similarly, no standardisation is found with award documents to the 1914 Iron Cross, and these may range from simple typewritten documents to formal documents. A selection is illustrated.

The total number of 1914 Iron Crosses First Class awarded will probably never be accurately known. Estimates vary between 80,000 and nearly a quarter of a million.

One interesting and oft disputed case was the award made to a young Gefreiter of 16 Bavarian Reserve Infantry Regiment-Adolf Hitler. Whilst few have disputed Hitler's right to the Iron Cross Second Class, many sources have doubted that he was awarded the Iron Cross First Class, some even claiming that it was awarded to him by Ludendorf, well after the war's conclusion, for political purposes. John Toland, however, in his scholarly biography of Hitler, has shown that Hitler was in fact recommended for the Iron Cross early in the war, but that the award was not confirmed, principally due to the fact that more names were put forward than there were awards available. Hitler was merely unlucky that his name was too far down the list. However, Hitler did receive the Iron Cross First Class, on 4 August 1918, for 'personal bravery and general merit'.

It is interesting to note, despite Allied propaganda which was understandably highly derogatory about him, that Hitler's personal bravery during World War One is a matter of record. His military decorations included both classes of Iron Cross, Military Cross Third Class with Swords, Wound Badge, Service Medal Third Class and the regimental diploma for outstanding bravery.

It is ironic that the officer making the award of the Iron Cross First Class to Adolf Hitler was his battalion adjutant, Oberleutnant Hugo Gutmann. Oberleutnant Gutmann was Jewish.

1914 IRON CROSS FIRST CLASS RECIPIENTS

Leutnant Fritz Nagel Fritz Nagel was a reserve Leutnant, serving with a motorised anti-aircraft unit during World War One. Already a holder of the Iron Cross Second Class, he was awarded the First Class for his part in the fighting in Albert, a small French town of some 7500 inhabitants. In command of a small mobile truck mounted Flak unit, Nagel was instructed to attempt to drive off ground attacks by aircraft of the Royal Flying Corps on German forces in the area. Whilst the legendary Manfred von Richthofen and his fighters battled with allied aircraft high in the skies

Leutnant der Reserve Fritz Nagel photographed in 1918 after the award of his Iron Cross First Class.

Unteroffizier Georg Maier, after the award of the Iron Cross for the action at Vouziers.

above Albert, low level attacks by other allied aircraft were causing heavy German casualties.

On entering Albert, Nagel encountered units of 1 Marine Infanterie Regiment and learned that parts of the town were still held by allied troops, and attempts to storm their positions were resulting in heavy casualties. It was decided to use Nagel's Flak gun in a ground support role against the allied machine gun nests. This was a very dangerous venture which would leave the gun crew, especially the driver, exposed to enemy small arms fire.

The attack, however, was a success and, miraculously, apart from a minor leg wound to one of the gunners, no one was injured. The driver, a former racing car driver, was awarded the Iron Cross First Class for his gallantry. The next day, Nagel's gun was again successful, shooting down a British Bristol F2B fighter during an air attack on Albert.

Shortly afterwards, Nagel discovered that the Commander of 3 Battalion, 1 Marine Infanterie Regiment had commended the bravery of Nagel and his men, and on 1 April 1918 Nagel was handed the following message:

Command of 23 Reserve Corps

Headquarters 1 April 1918

In the name of His Majesty the Emperor and King, I am decorating Leutnant der Reserve Nagel, of K Flak 82, with the Iron Cross First Class.

Signed,

General der Infanterie

Unteroffizier Georg Maier Georg Maier had served part of his war in Germany's Kaiserliche Marine as a crew member of U-55, winning the Iron Cross Second Class in 1917. In that same year he transferred to the army, joining 3 Machine Gun Company of 1 Bavarian Infantry Regiment.

On 21 October 1918, Maier's unit was just east of Vouziers on the Aisne River, and with only fifty men and four machine guns, fought off nine different attacks by troops of General Gourauds Fourth French Army. Although French troops at times reached within 50 metres of the German positions, the tenacity of the German defences always threw them back.

Attempts were then made to infiltrate snipers to attack the Germans, and Maier was responsible for eliminating three French snipers in one day.

On 25 October after the successful defence of their positions, things relaxed enough for the issue of wine and chocolates to the surviving troops, a rare luxury at that point in the war. As Maier and his best friend celebrated their success and their survival, tucking into their chocolate, a shot rang out and Maier's friend fell dead, shot through the throat by a French sniper.

Maier was later awarded the Iron Cross First Class for his service during these hectic few days. His regimental commander, Major von Schmidtler, received the coveted *Pour le Mérite*.

Maier survived the war and now lives in Gibsonia, Pennsylvania, USA.

THE 1914 BAR TO THE IRON CROSS OF 1870

Instituted on 4 June 1915 by Kaiser Wilhelm II to recognise those who had won the Iron Cross during the Franco-Prussian War, and had then further distinguished themselves during World War One, the 1914 Bar to

Obverse and reverse of the 1870 Iron Cross Second Class, an exceedingly rare piece indeed, showing the 25 Anniversary Oakleaves and the 1914 Bar.

the 1870 Iron Cross consists of a silver rectangular bar measuring 33 by 7.5mm in the centre of which is superimposed a small Iron Cross measuring 12.5mm. The bar was worn on the ribbon of the 1870 Iron Cross Second Class, just above the 25 Anniversary Oakleaves.

Even if one were to assume extreme youth in a winner of the 1870 Iron Cross, say eighteen years of age, then the recipient would be sixty three years old by the time the bar was instituted. Those still serving at this age would be very senior officers, so the number of bars awarded must have been very small indeed, and consequently the 1914 Bar to the 1870 Iron Cross is one of the scarcest German decorations of this period.

THE HILDEGARD ORDER

The South West African campaigns of World War One saw some important battles yet these received very little publicity compared to those of the European conflict. It was, however, in these very colonies that, on 13 September 1914, the first shots of the war were fired.

Following a victory by the German Schutztruppe on 23 September 1914, the German governor, Seitz, and the Schutztruppe commander, Oberstleutnant Heydebreck, met in Windhaek to discuss the production of a gallantry award which could be presented to soldiers of the Schutztruppe until such time as they returned to the Fatherland and could be presented with a formal decoration. Seitz suggested that his wife and other members of the overseas section of the German Red Cross should produce an embroidered cross and this suggestion was accepted by Heydebreck who was subsequently decorated along with nine of his men. This award, named the Hildegard Orden in honour of Governor Seitz's wife, Frau Hildegard Seitz, consisted of a black cloth cross in the same shape as the Iron Cross, with a silver grey or white thread border.

According to Dr K G Klietmann, the foremost authority on German decorations, only one example of this rare award has ever gone on public display, at the German Colonial Exhibition in Dresden in 1939. It must be considered therefore that the possibility of an original example of this decoration appearing now is very remote indeed.

The Grand Cross of the Iron Cross of 1914

The 1914 Grand Cross is virtually identical to its 1870 counterpart, differing only in the alteration to the date in the lower arm. Although all Grand Crosses feature genuine silver frames, the 1914 example was the first to be commonly marked with the silver content stamp, usually '900'. The overall size of the Grand Cross is 62mm.

An unexplained number of variants of the 1914 Grand Cross exist. This is strange considering the small number of awards which were made. The principal variants known are as follows:

1. Similar to the standard Grand Cross, but with only two acorns on the oak stem rather than the usual four.
2. As above, but having a ribbon ring suspension identical to that for the second class.
3. An apparently commemorative piece, having a blank reverse provided, presumably, to accommodate an inscription.

Only five awards of the 1914 Grand Cross were made, one of those being to the Kaiser himself. This was worn at the specific request of his

A fine original example of the 1914 Grand Cross. Note the rather rough finish to the paintwork.

The reverse view of the 1914 Grand Cross. Note that the original 1813 design has been retained.

Generals. A number of copies of the Grand Cross were made during both the Imperial and Third Reich periods for patriotic museum displays, shop window displays for medal retailers, etc, so that the number of pieces which exist far exceeds the number of awards made.

Kaiser Wilhelm II. Note that the Grand Cross is worn under the *Pour le Mérite*.

Opposite
Generalfeldmarschall von Hindenburg, centre, wearing his Grand Cross. The Breast Star is also partly visible. To the right can be seen Generalfeldmarschall von Mackensen wearing the traditional fur Pelmutze of the Hussar Regiments. Both carry their marshall's batons. To the extreme right is General Ludendorf.

THE 1914 GRAND CROSS RECIPIENTS

Generalfeldmarschall Paul Ludwig von Hindenburg Born in Posen in 1847, Hindenburg was to become one of Germany's greatest soldiers, and only the second man in history to win the Star to the Grand Cross.

At the age of only nineteen, Hindenburg saw action against the Austrian army at Königgratz in 1866, and later, in the Franco-Prussian war, fought at Metz and Sedan, and was present at the fall of Paris.

In 1914, Hindenburg was given a command on the Eastern Front and distinguished himself with victories at Tannenberg and Ivangorod. A year later, in conjunction with von Mackensen, he was instrumental in driving the Russians out of Poland. In 1916, Hindenburg was responsible for yet another important victory in the east against the Rumanians who had just declared war against the Central Powers. For this he was made the first recipient of the 1914 Grand Cross of the Iron Cross. The award was made on 9 December 1916.

In 1917, Hindenburg was appointed supreme commander of the German Army, subordinate only to the Kaiser himself. Following Germany's surrender in 1918, and the abdication of the Kaiser, it might have been expected that Hindenburg's career would be over. The situation

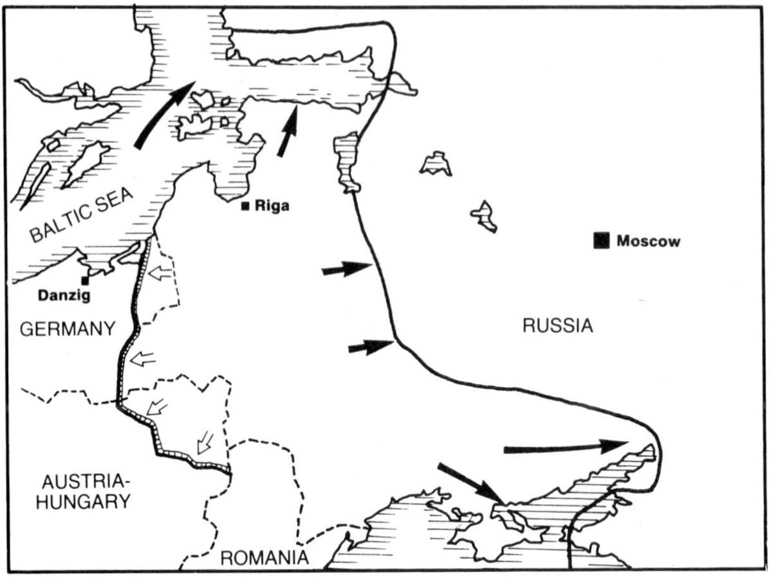

The Eastern Front in World War One, showing the fullest extent of both German and Russian advances.

of Germany having surrendered without having been comprehensively beaten on the battlefield, and without enemy troops having taken German soil, meant that many of the great military leaders still held the respect of the population. In 1925, Hindenburg became president, surviving re-election in 1932, his popularity as high as ever.

After the dismissal of Brüning as chancellor in 1932, Hindenburg, increasingly worried over the rise of Communism in Germany, began to look more favourably on Hitler's National Socialist German Workers Party, the Nazis, and named Hitler chancellor after the Party's election successes, in 1933.

Paul Ludwing von Hindenburg died in August 1934, and as befitting his life of service to his country, was given a hero's funeral.

General der Infanterie Erich Ludendorf Born, like Hindenburg, in Posen, but eighteen years his junior, Ludendorf's early military career was highly successful. He joined the army in 1873 and by 1894 was a General Staff Officer.

At the start of World War One, Ludendorf was assigned as Chief of Staff to Hindenburg, but whilst Hindenburg's greatest successes were on the

General aer Infanterie Erich Ludendorf. In this case, the Grand Cross is worn under and at the same level as the *Pour le Mérite*.

East Front, Ludendorf's war was spent mainly in the West, one of his greatest triumphs being against the Italians at Caporetto. Ludendorf received his Grand Cross of the Iron Cross in March 1918, in recognition of his successes in the West against British and French armies.

A right wing reactionary, Ludendorf supported the rise to power of the National Socialists, and took part in the abortive Munich Putsch. He subsequently served in the Reichstag. Ludendorf died in 1937. Ironically, in view of his earlier career, he had by this time become a pacifist.

Generalfeldmarschall Prinz Maximillian Joseph Maris Arnuf Leopold Born in 1846, Prince Leopold of Bavaria was the only Prince of the Royal Blood to win the 1914 Grand Cross. It was awarded to him in March 1918 in recognition of his leadership in command of the German 9 Army on the East Front, and for the capture of Warsaw in 1915. He died in 1930 at the age of eighty-four.

Generalfeldmarschall August von Mackensen A contemporary of Hindenburg, and only two years his junior, Mackensen made his name during the Franco-Prussian War, though his rise to fame came in 1915 when, with Hindenburg, he was responsible for driving the Russians out of Poland, and capturing Lwow. Mackensen in fact spent most of the war on the East Front, campaigning also against Rumania and Serbia. He received the Grand Cross in January 1917.

Though he retired in 1920, Mackensen by no means dropped out of public life, and many photographs of military occasions during the 1930s show him resplendent in his Imperial Hussars uniform complete with its deaths head Busby. Mackensen was further honoured by the Wehrmacht in December 1944, on his ninety-fifth birthday, by the bestowal of his name as an honour title on Kavallerie Regiment 5.

THE STAR TO THE GRAND CROSS OF THE IRON CROSS OF 1914

This award consists of an eight-pointed radiant star 88mm in diameter. It is crafted in genuine silver, and gilded. In the centre is affixed a standard Iron Cross First Class. Attachment was by means of a single vertical, flat, hinged pin, and a hook on each of the horizontal arms of the star.

This attractive award was presented only once, to Generalfeldmarschall von Hindenburg in recognition of his command during the last great German offensive in 1918. Together with the Star came a personal letter of commendation and thanks from the Kaiser.

It is known that Hindenburg had two specimens of the Star. One remained with the Generalfeldmarschall's family until at least 1945 after which it disappeared somewhere into the East. The other example was given by Hindenburg to an officer who was at the time serving with the Armistice Committee. On the death of this officer, his collection was purchased by an East European collector. Both examples of the Star are now therefore beind the 'Iron Curtain' and are unlikely to be seen again in the West. However, several contemporary museum copies were produced, and occasionally appear. These feature a variety of construction methods. The example which is illustrated has the Iron Cross affixed by means of a large single screw plate, whilst others feature four small screws.

Right
The 1914 Star to the Grand Cross of the Iron Cross. This is an original contemporary copy — the real 'Hindenburgstern' is in Eastern Europe.

Opposite left
Generalfeldmarschall von Mackensen, wearing the *Pour le Mérite.*

Opposite right
Generalfeldmarschall Prince Leopold of Bavaria. This photograph was taken before the award of the Grand Cross.

THE IRON CROSS OF 1939

The background to the outbreak of World War Two has been studied and analysed countless times in recent years, so it would be wasteful of space to look at this period in depth once again.

However, from the point of view of the history of the Iron Cross, it is interesting to reflect that the German Army did not suffer a conclusive defeat on the battlefield during World War One. Armistice terms were agreed, but formal surrender did not follow until much later. The German forces were removed from the battlefield, and the war weary soldiers sent home. Many were extremely dismayed to return home, tired but still feeling undefeated, only to find terrible conditions: unemployment, inflation, corruption, riots and near anarchy. After their sacrifices at the front, many soldiers were furious at what they considered to be a betrayal by the politicians at home. The 'stab in the back theory' quickly took root, and it was only to be a matter of time before the weak Weimar Republic found itself in dire straits.

Disillusioned soldiers drifted into the ultra right wing Freikorps movements which battled openly with the communists on the streets. Freikorps men who were arrested found sympathisers in the German police and the sentences passed against them were almost always very light, whilst the communists were jailed.

The rise of Hitler's National Socialists with their military style uniforms and regalia in the early 1930s attracted many former soldiers. Photographs from this period show many Party members and Freikorps men proudly wearing their decorations from World War One. In fact, the awarding of

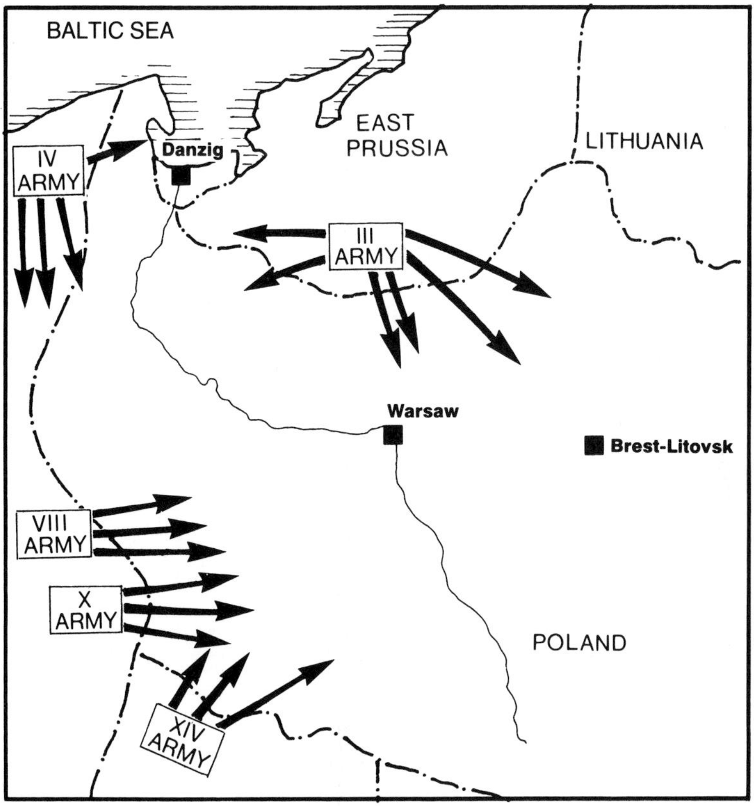

The disposition of the main German forces for the invasion of Poland, during the course of which the first Iron Crosses of World War Two were won.

Heinz Macher with men of his Pioniere Kompanie on the Russian Front in 1943.

Iron Crosses for actions during the war continued for several years after 1918.

The rise of Adolf Hitler to power in Germany gave many ex-servicemen a figurehead who appealed greatly to them. He was, after all, a former 'common soldier' who had been decorated for gallantry on the Western Front. Once in power, he rapidly brought down inflation, reduced unemployment and banished the communists. The average man in the street was content to turn a blind eye to the more sinister aspects of the Nazi regime in view of the many benefits it had already brought to the country.

Hitler was a very astute judge of the psychological benefits to be had from military symbolism. Almost every Nazi organisation had its own particular uniform and accoutrements. The Freikorps movement and the various ex-servicemen's organisations were quickly absorbed into the appropriate Nazi units. Although the world in general had considered Germany to have been a defeated nation not too many Germans agreed, and military decorations still held great significance and were openly worn.

Meanwhile, the Reichswehr of the Weimar Republic had been greatly expanded by Hitler and, although few were in any way fervent Party supporters, senior military men were certainly not vehemently opposed to him. Many undoubtedly saw him as the lesser of two evils. He had, after all, disposed of the communists and rebuilt the army, and many senior officers no doubt felt that Hitler himself could be disposed of later once he had 'served his purpose'.

However, Hitler was far more clever than they gave him credit for being. When he re-occupied the Rhineland against their advice, he was proved right and them wrong. Again, he occupied Austria, took Memel, and then the Sudetenland, and each time his military advisors warned against such action, and each time they were proved wrong. The military became less and less inclined to oppose him.

When Germany, rearmed and powerful once more, poised to invade Poland in September 1939, Hitler once again instituted the Iron Cross, in a much simplified form which bore only the institution dates and the swastika. The ordinary German soldier, encouraged by Hitler's 'bloodless' victories in the past, no doubt looked forward to short, glorious campaigns and great victories, little forseeing the carnage that the coming war would bring and with it Germany's utter devastation.

The Iron Cross was renewed by Adolf Hitler on 1 September 1939. The document read as follows.

After arriving at the conclusion that the German people must be called to arms in defence of an imminent attack, I will renew for the sons of Germany, as in the past great wars in the defence of the home and the Fatherland, the Order of the Iron Cross.

Article 1

The Iron Cross will be awarded in the following classes:

Iron Cross Second Class

Iron Cross First Class

Knights Cross of the Iron Cross

Knights Cross of the Iron Cross with Oakleaves

Grand Cross of the Iron Cross

Article 2

- i The Iron Cross will be awarded for outstanding service to service personnel and for bravery in the face of the enemy.
- ii The cross for a higher class must be preceeded by that of a lower class.

Article 3

The awarding of the Grand Cross depends upon my own decision for outstanding deeds which are decisive. Articles 1 and 4 state that the Iron Cross has the following classes and, is awarded in this order: Second Class, First Class, Knights Cross, and Grand Cross.

Article 4

- i The Iron cross First and Second Class are the same as for those in World War One, except that there is on the face a swastika and the year 1939. The reverse of the Second Class has the year 1813. The Second Class is worn on a black, white and red ribbon on the medal bar or in the buttonhole. The First Class is worn without a ribbon on the left breast.
- ii The Knights Cross is larger than the Iron Cross Second Class. It is worn on a black, white and red ribbon around the neck.
- iii The Oakleaves to the Knights Cross of the Iron Cross consist of three silver oakleaves on the ribbon clip.
- iv The Grand Cross is twice the size of the Iron Cross Second Class and is worn on a wide black, white and red ribbon around the neck.

Article 5

The holder of either class of the Iron Cross of World War One who distinguishes himself will receive a silver clasp with an eagle (wings out) holding a wreath and swastika and the year 1939 which will be worn on the ribbon in the case of the Second Class and pinned above the Cross on the left breast in the case of the First Class.

Article 6

The award will be accompanied by a possession certificate.

Article 7

The Iron Cross in case of death will be returned to the next of kin at the family home.

Article 8

The Headquarters of the Chief of the Army High Command, Reichsminister, with the Minister of State and Chief of the Presiding Council,

Berlin, 1 September 1939

Der Führer (Adolf Hitler)

Chief of Army High Command (Keitel)

Reichsminister of Interior (Frick)

Minister of State, Chancellery Chief, Head and Reichs Councillor (Dr Meissner)

The Iron Cross Second Class of 1939

The Iron Cross Second Class of 1939 is similar in its design and construction to its earlier counterparts, being the usual blackened iron centre in a silver frame. In the case of the 1939 piece, however, genuine silver is the exception rather than the rule, most frames being in silver plate.

The obverse centre features a swastika with, in the lower arm, the institution date, 1939. The reverse is rather more plain than on earlier pieces, featuring only the original institution date, 1813, in the lower arm. The overall size is around 43mm, the silvered frame being 4mm wide.

The 1939 Iron Cross Second Class was suspended from a 30mm wide ribbon similar to that of earlier issues, but with the colour of the central portion changed to red, thus reflecting the national colours of the Third Reich.

The award was presented in a small blue paper or fawn paper packet with the title of the awarded printed on it in black Gothic characters. Occasional examples appear in fitted presentation cases and it is assumed that these were for award to higher ranking recipients.

Somewhere around 5 Million awards were made between 1939 and 1945, a huge number by any standards. At the start of World War Two,

the Iron Cross Second Class was still regarded quite highly, but as the war progressed and awards were made *en masse* to entire units, this decoration came to be regarded with scorn by many front line soldiers. Large numbers were also awarded to non-military personnel such as Railway Police, Labour Corps, Hitler Youth, Merchant Navy, etc.

No special Non-Combatant ribbon was produced for the 1939 Iron Cross, the institution of the Kriegs Verdienst Kreuz (War Merit Cross) precluding the need for such a ribbon. The ribbon for the War Merit Cross was in fact the same as for the Iron Cross, but with the colours reversed in the tradition of earlier non-combatant Iron Cross ribbons.

The War Merit Cross was intended for award to those who had performed meritorious service in aid of the war effort, and was awarded with swords for military personnel. There are several cases on record where deeds which one might have supposed would be rewarded by the Iron Cross received the War Merit Cross, and vice versa. One particular example of the latter is Flugkapitän Hanna Reitsch. This famous personality was a skilled test pilot, and her bravery cannot be doubted. It appears, however, that as she was not a member of the armed forces, the War Merit Cross would have been an apt award in her case. In any case her awards were not for combat action. Yet she was awarded both classes of the Iron Cross.

Right
A rare example of the 1939 Iron Cross Second Class in its fitted presentation case.

Opposite left
The Iron Cross Second Class of 1939. The manufacturer's code is stamped on the suspension ring.

Opposite right
Reverse of the 1939 Iron Cross Second Class.

There are also cases of military personnel, serving at the front under combat conditions (ie Tank Repair Mechanics, Supply Troops, etc) receiving the War Merit Cross when a case could well have been made for the award of the Iron Cross. It can be seen therefore that there seems to have been a certain amount of overlap in the awarding of Merit and Iron Crosses.

1939 IRON CROSS SECOND CLASS RECIPIENTS

Captain Otto Giese Otto Giese served as Second Mate on the *Anneliese Essberber.* His principal duties were navigation, demolitions, signals deciphering and, importantly, liaison officer with the Kriegsmarine. The *Anneliese Essberber* was a merchant supply ship, and had been a support vessel for the Raider 'Ship 45', better known as the *Komet.*

Anneliese Essberber had left Yokohama, Japan, at the beginning of June 1941, bound for Bordeaux. She was camouflaged as the Japanese freighter *Ryoku Maru* of Osaka Shosen Kaisha and had supplied *Komet,* whilst en route to Bordeaux, in the Pacific. On reaching the Atlantic, she was recamouflaged as the Norwegian merchantman *Herstein* of Herlafson Sigurd & Co. in Oslo.

Anneliese Essberber safely reached home waters on 9 November 1941 and for his part in this highly successful trip and breach of the allied blockade, Otto Giese was awarded the Iron Cross Second Class. The Iron Cross was attached to Otto Giese's uniform by Admiral Menche who, at Giese's request, arranged his transfer to the U-Boat service where he served for the rest of the war, seeing action in the North Sea, North Atlantic, South Atlantic and Indian Oceans.

Captain Giese survived the war and now lives in retirement in the USA.

Otto Giese wearing the Iron Cross Second Class immediately after its award by Admiral Menche.

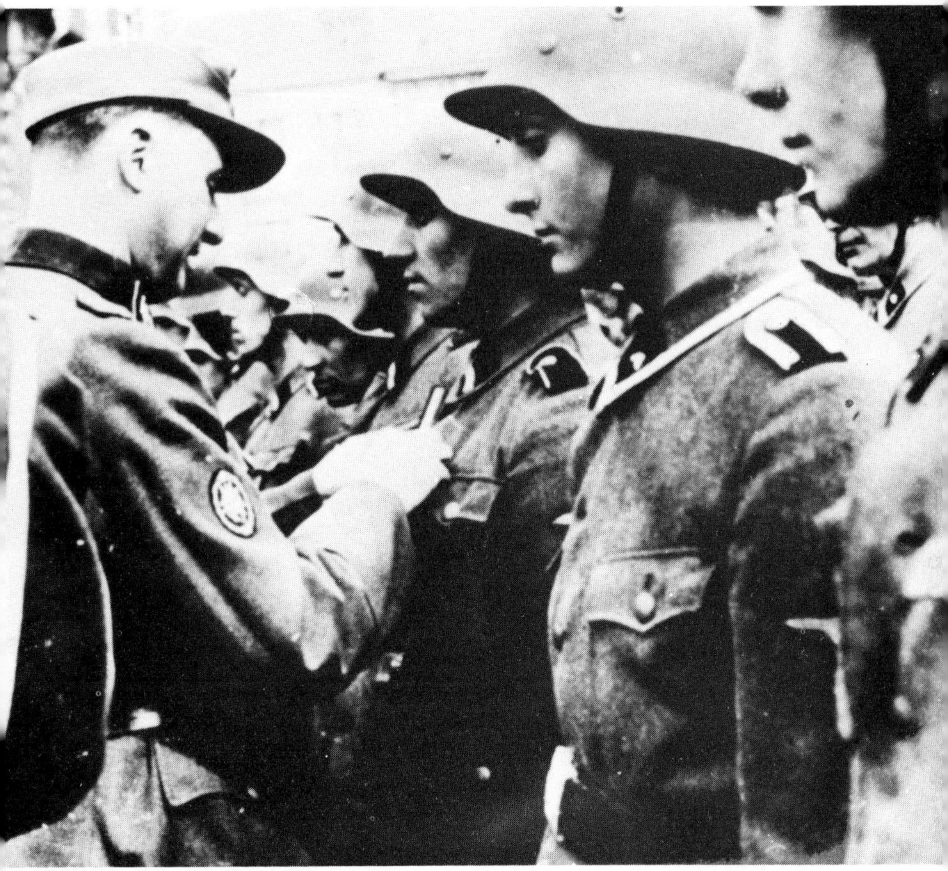

SS-Sturmbannführer Leon Degrelle awards the Iron Cross Second Class to men of 28 SS-Sturmbrigade.

A young seaman receives the Iron Cross from Knight's Cross winner Kapitän zur See Erdmenger, the commander of 8 Destroyer Flotilla.

Opposite
An officer and young NCO of the Reichsarbeitsdienst wearing newly awarded Iron Crosses.

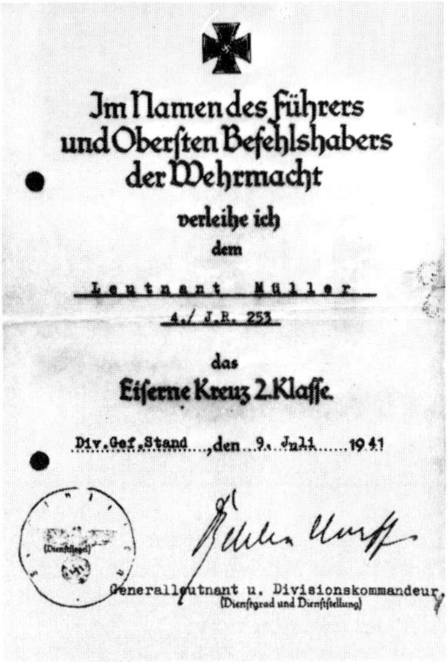
Im Namen des Führers
und Obersten Befehlshabers
der Wehrmacht
verleihe ich
dem
Leutnant Müller
4./I.R. 253
das
Eiserne Kreuz 2.Klasse.
Div.Gef.Stand...,den..9. Juli......1941
Generalleutnant u. Divisionskommandeur
(Dienstgrad und Dienststellung)

The award document for the Iron Cross Second Class to a Leutnant in 253 Infantry Regiment. Müller had served in the Allgemeine-SS before the war.

Schutzstaffeln der N.S.D.A.P.
SS-Führer-
Ausweis Nr. 4 700
Pg. Müller, Georg
Mitglieds-Nr. 46 581
ist SS-Untersturmführer
in der Stammabt.West Bez.25
Georg Müller
Eigenhändige Unterschrift

Leutnant Muller's pre-war SS identity card.

THE 1939 BAR TO THE IRON CROSS SECOND CLASS OF 1914

Founded on 1 September 1939, the Bar to the Iron Cross was intended to reward those who had been decorated with the Iron Cross during World War One and who had then further distinguished themselves during World War Two.

The Second Class Bar consists of an eagle with short outstretched wings, clutching a wreathed swastika. Beneath the swastika was a small rectangular bar bearing the date 1939. On the reverse are four prongs which push through the ribbon of the 1914 Iron Cross Second Class to hold the bar in place. It was worn on the Second Class ribbon, from the buttonhole, in the usual manner.

Its overall size is 30 by 39mm, though one major variant exists

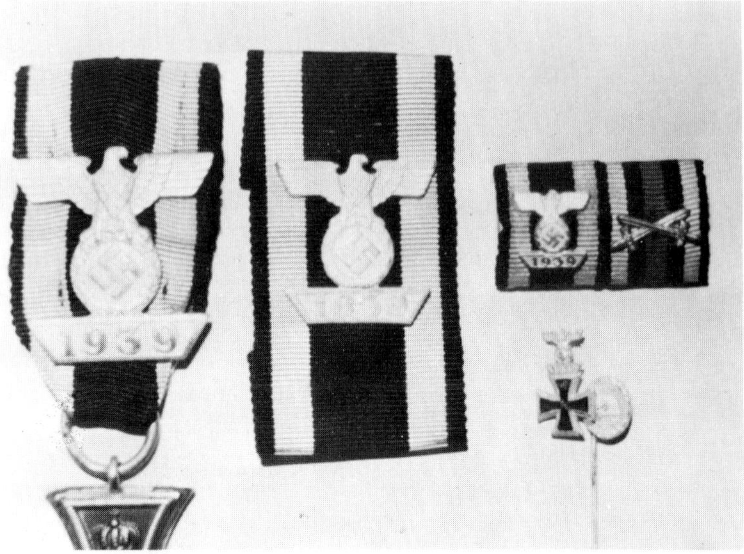

Left to right: standard award pattern Second Class Bar; smaller size full dress formal version; ribbon bar miniature, and stick pin miniature.

Opposite left
The standard pattern 1939 Iron Cross First Class.

Opposite right
Reverse of the Iron Cross First Class of 1939 showing the typical pin fitting.

The Iron Cross Second Class of 1914 with the 1939 Bar attached. Normally, only the bar on the ribbon would be worn from the buttonhole.

measuring only 25 by 25mm. This was intended for wear on the medal ribbon when the medal itself was worn on formal dress occasions. It is of much finer manufacture than the full size version, and has only two prongs on the reverse. It was available through retail channels and had to be purchased at the wearer's own expense.

The Bar to the Iron Cross Second Class was normally awarded in a small brown or blue paper packet with the title of the award printed in black Gothic script.

The Iron Cross First Class of 1939

Unlike its earlier predecessors, the 1939 Iron Cross First Class was a highly standardised piece, with only a small number of minor variants produced. The obverse design is identical to that of the Second Class, whilst the reverse is plain with a vertical, flat, hinged pin attachment. Materials used were generally iron for the centre and silver plate for the frame. The First Class Iron Cross was presented in a small black box with the outline of the Iron Cross impressed into its lid in silver. The

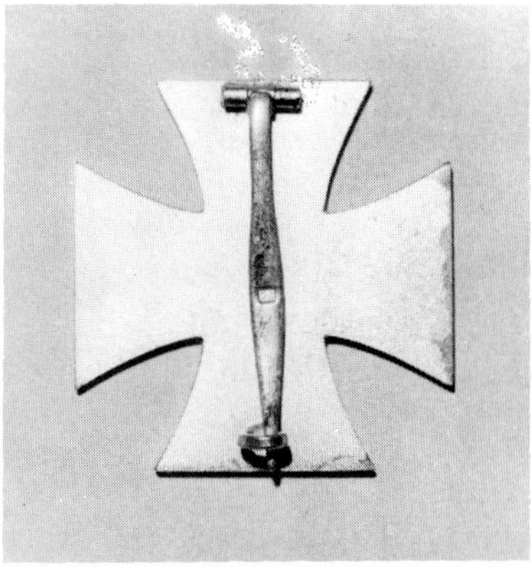

lining was in white satin to the lid, and white velvet or flock to the base.

The variants to the 1939 First Class were very minor and reflect only manufacturers' fashions. These variants commonly encountered include the following:

1. As the standard type but with a screwback fitting to the reverse.
2. As the standard type, but slightly convex.
3. A rare version, slightly smaller than normal at around 41 by 41mm and with narrower arms. This type was made by the Berlin firm of Godet.
4. As with 1 or 2, but with brass rather than iron used for the centre.

Although rare, cloth versions of the 1939 First Class are known. Generally, they are rather crude and were not at all popular.

Opposite left
The most common variant to the 1939 First Class Iron Cross was the Screwback, shown here.

Opposite right
Reverse of the Screwback Iron Cross First Class. Note the maker's code L/50 stamped at the foot of the lower arm.

Opposite
A group of minesweeper crewmen parade on the award of the Iron Cross First Class.

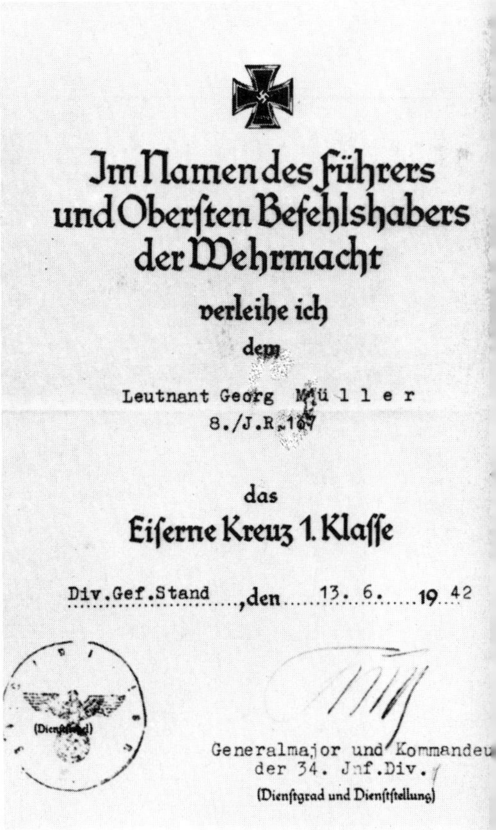

Im Namen des Führers
und Obersten Befehlshabers
der Wehrmacht

verleihe ich

dem

Leutnant Georg Müller
8./J.R.107

das

Eiserne Kreuz 1. Klasse

Div.Gef.Stand, den 13. 6. 1942

Generalmajor und Kommandeur
der 34. Jnf.Div.
(Dienstgrad und Dienststellung)

Right
The award document for the 1939 Iron Cross First Class. Examples were also made with block letters rather than Gothic script.

A very rare cloth version was also produced. Apparently privately purchased and unofficial, this version can not have been very popular, judging by the lack of photographic evidence of its wear and the very few examples which have survived.

Around 750,000 Iron Crosses First Class are thought to have been awarded between 1939 and 1945.

A young paratrooper wears the Iron Cross First and Second Classes. The way in which the Second Class is worn suggests that it has just been awarded in which case the First Class must have been worn at the same time, an uncommon though not unknown event.

Opposite
A group of NCO's from the elite 'Grossdeutschland' Division are presented with the First Class Iron Cross.

1939 IRON CROSS FIRST CLASS RECIPIENTS

Torpedo-Obermechaniker Heinrich Böhm Born in Gross-Zimmern, Heinrich Böhm had a varied career in the Kriegsmarine. He served for a brief period on the pocket battleship *Admiral Graf Spee* as a torpedo mechanic before transferring to the destroyer service, where he was posted to *Z17,* the *Diether von Roeder,* a 2400-tonner with a crew of over 300. *Diether von Roeder* carried out several pre-war goodwill cruises, and after the start of World War Two saw heavy action at the Battle of Narvik where she was so badly damaged that she had to be scuttled. Over one-third of her crew were killed.

For his part in the Narvik action, Heinrich Böhm received the Narvik Shield in Gold, the Destroyer War Badge, and the Iron Cross Second Class. *Diether von Roeder* was sunk on 13 April 1940, and the award of the Iron Cross came on 15 May, but the Narvik Shield and Destroyer War Badge were not awarded until November of that year.

After the loss of his ship, Heinrich Böhm transferred to the U-Boat service and, after completing his training, was assigned to *U-377* under Otto Köhler's command. Qualifying for his U-Boat badge on 2 June 1942 after three operational cruises against the enemy, Böhm went on to win the

Torpedoobermechaniker Heinrich Böhm. A veteran of the *Graf Spee* and the destroyer *Diether von Roeder,* Böhm won the rare U-Boat Combat Clasp in Bronze during his service in *U-377.*

Opposite
Kapitän zur See Otto Köhler, commander of *U-377.* The Iron Cross First Class is worn on the U-Boat blouse.

Below
Heinrich Böhm, on the right, is wearing the Iron Cross First Class, Narvik Shield, U-Boat Badge and the Destroyer's War Badge. At the time of this photograph, Böhm held the rank of petty officer.

Iron Cross First Class in October 1943. When Otto Köhler gave up his command to take up a shore posting at a Torpedo Training School, Böhm, as an experienced torpedo mechanic, was invited to go with him. This saved Böhm's life, as *U-377* was lost in action shortly afterwards.

Böhm was subsequently awarded the U-Boat Clasp in Bronze in November 1944 in recognition of his service on *U-377*, one of the few recipients of this rare badge. Heinrich Böhm ended the war as a Torpedo Obermechaniker, a warrant officer grade, and now lives in retirement in his home town.

Stabsobermaschinist Jakob Mallmann Born in Köln-Lindenthal in July 1914, Jakob Mallmann joined the new Reichsmarine in April 1933 at the age of nineteen. Initially, he served on minesweepers before attending Engineering Schools for trade training. Following this he attended the U-Boat School at Pillau on the Baltic for specialist training as a U-Boat diesel mechanic.

As a trained U-Boat engineer, Mallmann was then posted to a Marineunteroffiziervorschule (Naval NCO Training School) and on completion of this course joined the crew of *U-34.*

The rapidly expanding U-Boat service was soon to be joined by a new vessel, *U-377,* being constructed at the Howaldtswerke wharf in Kiel, and Jakob Mallmann joined her crew shortly before she was launched in August 1941. *U-377* was commissioned on 1 October 1941 under Kapitänleutnant Otto Köhler and, after trials in the Baltic, left for her first combat mission in February 1942.

U-377 had a moderately successful start to her career, bringing the award of the Iron Cross Second Class to Jakob Mallmann during 1942. The award document was personally signed by the Commander-in-Chief U-Boats, Admiral Dönitz. On 24 March 1943, his Iron Cross Second Class was complemented by the First Class. At this point he had reached the rank of Obermaschinist, a warrant officer class two grading.

In April 1943, Otto Köhler handed over command of *U-377* to

Obermachinist Jakob Mallmann. This photograph was taken before the award of the Iron Cross First Class. The ribbon of the Second Class is worn at the buttonhole. The U-Boat Badge is also visible.

Opposite
Jakob Mallmann with crewmates from *U-377.* Note the U-Boat overalls, and the Iron Cross First Class worn on the battledress.

Oberleutnant zur See Gerhard Kluth. Shortly afterwards, on her twelfth mission, *U-377* was attacked on the surface by an RAF Coastal Command Liberator bomber. Two crew members were killed and Kluth was wounded.

On returning from this mission, Jak Mallmann, now a Stabsobermaschinist, was sent to Officer Training School to take his commission as an engineering officer. Unfortunately, his replacement in *U-377* was taken ill, and he was required to return to *U-377* for one last patrol, the thirteenth.

U-377 left Brest on 15 December 1943, and at 1544 hours a message was received from her at U-Boat Headquarters, stating her position as 46.10 N, 20.00 W. It was the last message ever received from her. *U-377* was never seen again. Only after the war was it discovered that *U-377* had been sunk by a torpedo from another U-Boat during an attack on an allied convoy. An extremely tragic and ironic death, to be killed, accidentally by his own side, on a vessels thirteenth mission, a mission on which he should never have sailed.

U-377 crewmen pose in typically casual U-Boat dress as *U-377* lies in Narvik Fjord. Jakob Mallmann is at the extreme right.

Opposite
Crew members of *U-377* relax on the conning tower. In the centre of the back row, heavily bearded, is Torpedoobermechaniker Heinrich Böhm.

SS-Obersturmbannführer Richard Schulze-Kossens Richard Schulze-Kossens, a Berliner born in 1914, joined the SS in 1934 and was trained at the SS Officer Training School at Bad Tölz in Bavaria, being commissioned into the elite Leibstandarte-SS 'Adolf Hitler' as an SS-Untersturmführer in 1936.

Before the outbreak of war, Schulze-Kossens was attached to the Foreign Office and accompanied Joachim von Ribbentrop, the German Foreign Minister to the signing of the Russo-German non-aggression pact in Moscow, meeting both Molotov and Stalin. He was also at the Berghof during Mussolini's state visit in 1937.

When war broke out, Schulze-Kossens served with the 'Leibstandarte' during the Polish campaign and the French campaign, before the opening of the assault on the Balkans, where he took part in the invasion of Greece and Jugoslavia. By the end of these campaigns, Schulze-Kossens had won both Second and First Class Iron Crosses.

In 1941, during the early days of the invasion of the Soviet Union, Schulze-Kossens' brother, Hansgeorg, was killed. Hansgeorg had been an adjutant on Hitler's staff and, when expressing his condolences to Schulze-

As adjutant to Adolf Hitler, Richard Schulze-Kossens stands behind as Hitler addresses newly commissioned officers of the Leibstandarte. The Iron Cross is worn on the left breast and the German Cross on the right.

SS-Sturmbannführer Richard Schulze, wearing the Iron Cross Second Class ribbon on the lapel, the First Class Iron Cross on the breast, and, above it, the Infantry Close Combat Clasp. He also wears the 'Adolf Hitler' cuffband on the left sleeve.

Richard Schulze-Kossens, as the SS-Obersturmbannführer and Commander of the Officer Training School at Bad Tölz, addresses his cadets in early 1945.

Kossens, Hitler offered him the same position. This was a golden opportunity for an up and coming young officer, and Schulze-Kossens joined Hitler's personal staff, becoming an orderly officer, and eventually a personal adjutant. In many wartime photographs of Hitler and his entourage, the tall figure of Richard Schulze-Kossens can be seen in the background.

In December 1944, Schulze-Kossens, a combat experienced officer bearing both Iron Crosses (and the German Cross in Gold) was given command of the Bad-Tölz Officer Training School where he himself had been trained. Eventually, in the closing stages of the war, he was tasked with raising a Combat Group (nominally a Division), 38 SS-Grenadier Division 'Nibelungen' from the staff and pupils of the school.

At the age of only thirty-one, Schulze-Kossens was an SS-Obersturmbannführer (lieutenant-colonel) and a divisional commander. His war came to an end when his unit surrendered to US Forces in May 1945.

Richard Schulze-Kossens now lives in retirement in Dusseldorf, and has written the definitive history of the Waffen-SS Officer Training Academies, *Militarischer Führernachwuchs der Waffen-SS — Die Junkerschulen* (Munin Verlag).

THE 1939 BAR TO THE IRON CROSS FIRST CLASS OF 1914

The First Class Bar is of the same basic design as the Second Class, but has a wider wingspan to the eagle, at 44mm. The reverse features a vertical

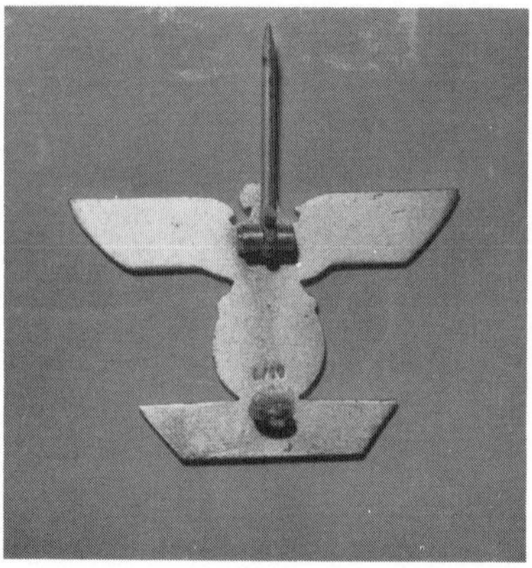

Reverse of the First Class Bar. This privately purchased replacement piece features the less usual needle type pin, and maker's code L/11.

The 1939 Bar to the 1914 Iron Cross First Class.

Reverse view of the standard issue Bar. Note the typical flat wide pin.

The case for the Bar to the Iron Cross First Class with its typical impressed motif of the award on the lid.

hinged pin instead of prongs and the Bar was pinned to the left breast of the tunic above the 1914 Iron Cross First Class. Both First Class and Second Class Bars were finished in an attractive matt silver oxide finish with the highlights polished.

Two major variants are known. The first has a screwback fitting on the reverse whilst the second, rarer version has the First Class Bar welded directly to the upper arm of a 1914 Iron Cross First Class. Both of these variants would be privately purchased by the wearer at his own expense.

The First Class Bar was presented in a small black case the lid of which had the design of the bar impressed into its surface in silver. The lid was lined with white silk, and the base with black velvet.

Approximately 100,000 Bars of both Classes were awarded.

Variant type of Bar, welded directly to the upper arm of the Iron Cross First Class. This type is rather rare and much sought after.

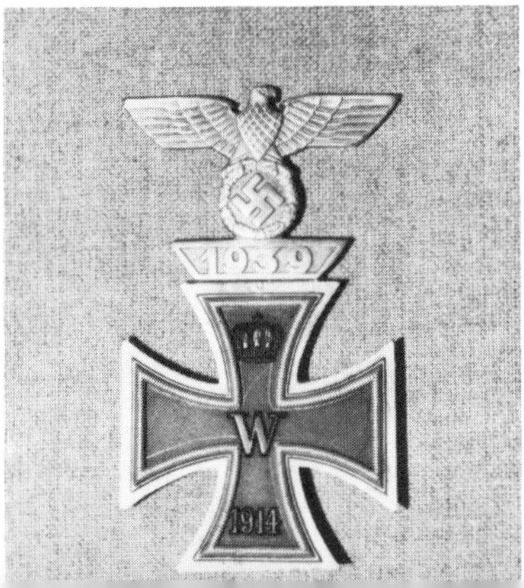

Reverse of the variant Bar. The Bar itself is devoid of any form of attachment device.

This Kapitän zur See of destroyers wears the Iron Cross First Class and, above that, the ribbon for the Second Class on the ribbon bar rather than in the buttonhole.

The Knight's Cross of the Iron Cross of 1939

Instituted on 1 September 1939, the Knight's Cross was a new award, intended to bridge the considerable gap which existed between the Iron Cross First Class, and the Grand Cross. It measures 48 by 55mm (including the eye for the ribbon loop) and consists of what is basically a smaller version of the Grand Cross. The obverse and reverse designs are identical to the Second Class, and the suspension loop is very similar to that for the Grand Cross. Also like the Grand Cross, it was worn at the neck. The frame of the Knight's Cross as awarded is genuine silver and is usually hallmarked on the reverse of the frame on the upper arm just below the eyelet. Some examples also carry maker's marks.

Very little variation will be encountered on the Knight's Cross, which was manufactured to very high standards. Many Knight's Cross winners puchased additional, or replacement specimens, through retail outlets. These examples often used alternative materials, such as silver plated zinc for the frame and brass for the centre. The use of brass or copper for the centre is said to have been popular with Kriegsmarine personnel, due to the non-rusting quality of these metals in salt air. The standard Knight's Cross is normally found to weigh between 30 and 33 grams, but this will not necessarily hold true for replacement specimens.

The Knight's Cross was suspended from a neck ribbon 45mm wide. A

A fine original example of the Knight's Cross of the Iron Cross. The frame's beaded edge is finished in an attractive matt silver oxide effect.

Reverse of the Knight's Cross. Below the eye for the ribbon loop is the '800' silver content stamp.

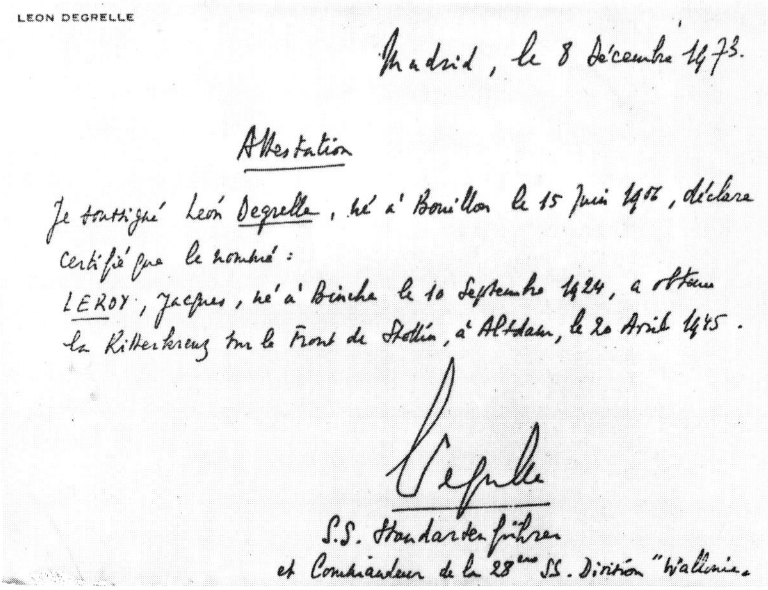
LEON DEGRELLE

Madrid, le 8 Décembre 1973.

Attestation

Je soussigné Léon Degrelle, né à Bouillon le 15 Juin 1906, déclare certifié que le nommé:
LEROY, Jacques, né à Binche le 10 Septembre 1924, a obtenu la Ritterkreuz sur le Front de Stettin, à Altdam, le 20 Avril 1945.

S.S. Standartenführer
et Commandeur de la 28ème SS. Division "Wallonie"

Above
Attestation, in French, signed by SS-Standartenführer Leon Degrelle, commander of the 'Wallonien' Division, confirming the award of the Knight's Cross to Jaques Leroy. The date of attestation is December 1973.

Bottom
Further attestation, in French, by the divisional adjutant supporting Degrelle's attestation to the award of Leroy's Knight's Cross in April 1945. Leroy's name is not to be found in the official lists of Knight's cross awards.

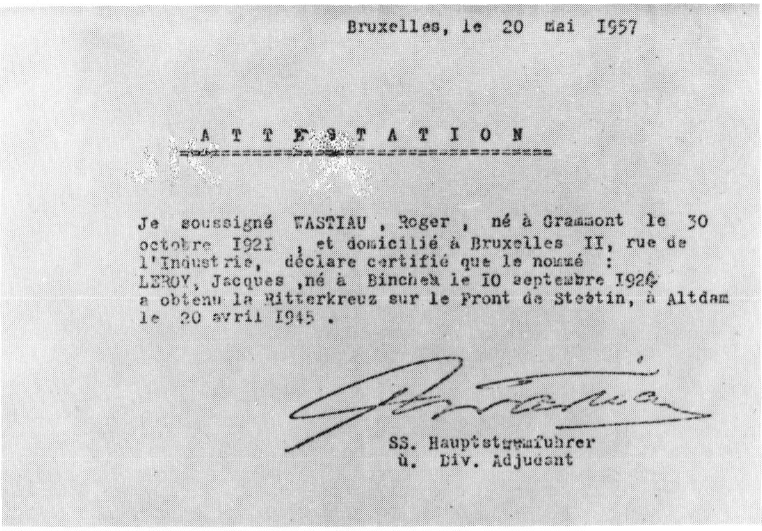
Bruxelles, le 20 mai 1957

A T T E S T A T I O N

Je soussigné WASTIAU, Roger, né à Grammont le 30 octobre 1921, et domicilié à Bruxelles II, rue de l'Industrie, déclare certifié que le nommé :
LEROY, Jacques, né à Binche le 10 septembre 1924
a obtenu la Ritterkreuz sur le Front de Stettin, à Altdam
le 20 avril 1945.

SS. Hauptsturmführer
u. Div. Adjudant

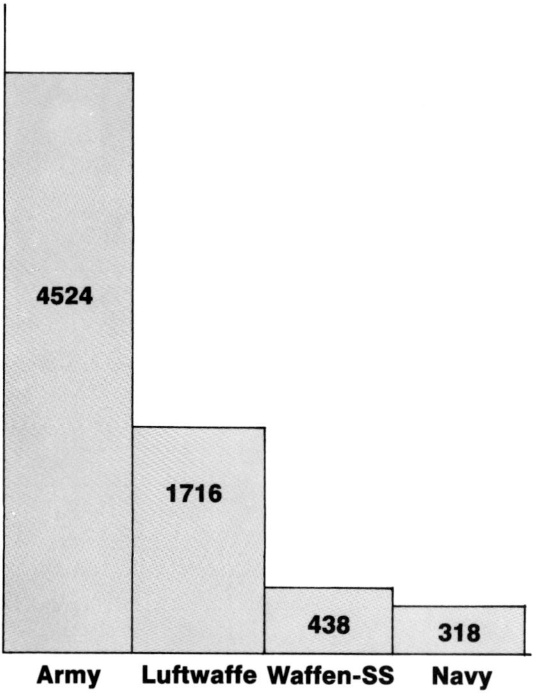

Distribution of the Knight's Cross by Arm of Service. Naturally, the army, with the greatest number of men under arms, has the largest number of awards. On a pro-rata basis, the awards are well distributed.

variety of methods was used to secure the ribbon, including ties, elastics, hooks and eyes, press studs, etc. This was left to the whim of the individual wearer.

The Knight's Cross was presented in a black case measuring approximately 155 by 85 by 27mm. The base was fitted to the shape of the Cross and covered in black velvet. The lid was lined with white satin.

It was not uncommon for Knight's Cross winners to wear a converted Iron Cross Second Class in place of the Knight's Cross, for fear of losing or damaging the original award.

Due to the chaotic conditions prevailing during the closing stages of the war, when numbers of recommendations for the award were made but never confirmed, the correct, accurate total of awards made may never be known. Many awards have only come to light following post-war research. Illustrated are examples of this; attestations by officers of the 28 SS-Freiwilligen Panzer Grenadier Division 'Wallonien' to the award of the

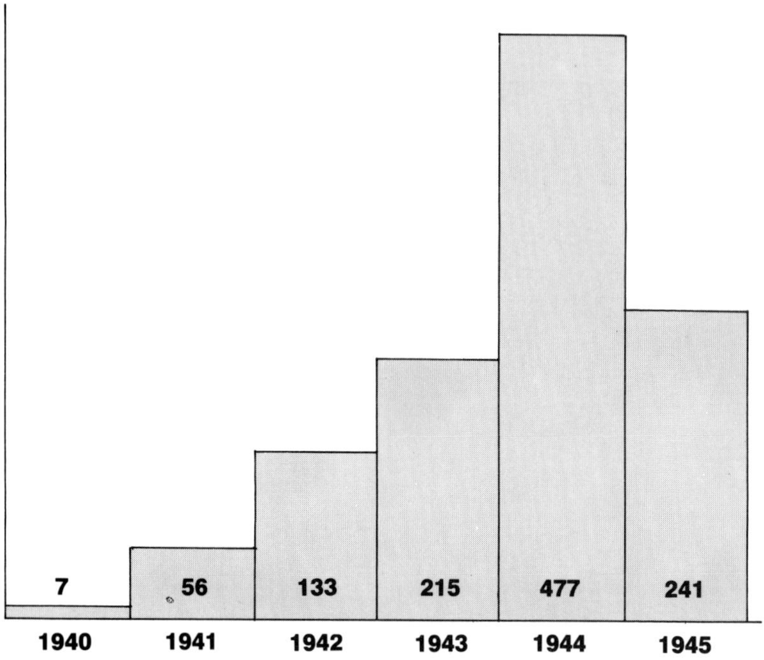

Knight's Cross to one of their men. These attestations are dated 1973.

The esteem in which the Knight's Cross was held has been perpetuated post-war by the Ordensgemeinschaft der Ritterkreuzträger (OdR), the Association of Knight's Cross Bearers. Today, the OdR has about 1050 members from the 1800 Knight's Cross bearers who are still alive. The Association produces a quarterly magazine, *Das Ritterkreuz* and holds national as well as regional reunions.

In wartime Germany, picture postcards of Knight's Cross winners were produced in large numbers and avidly collected by young Germans. Today, these photographs are sought after collectors' items, so much so that reproductions are now appearing, complete with the correct sepia tints to the photographs. There is no doubt that Knight's Cross winners were held in the highest respect by the public in wartime Germany, and many magazines contained stirring tales of their exploits. Even now, Ritterkreuzträger are highly respected members of the community.

The number of Knight's Crosses awarded was around 7318, with 890 Oakleaves, 159 Swords and twenty-seven 'Diamonds'. Many would find this number rather high for such a coveted award, but it must be remembered that when compared with, say, the United Kingdom, Germany did not have the wide range of Gallantry Awards which were

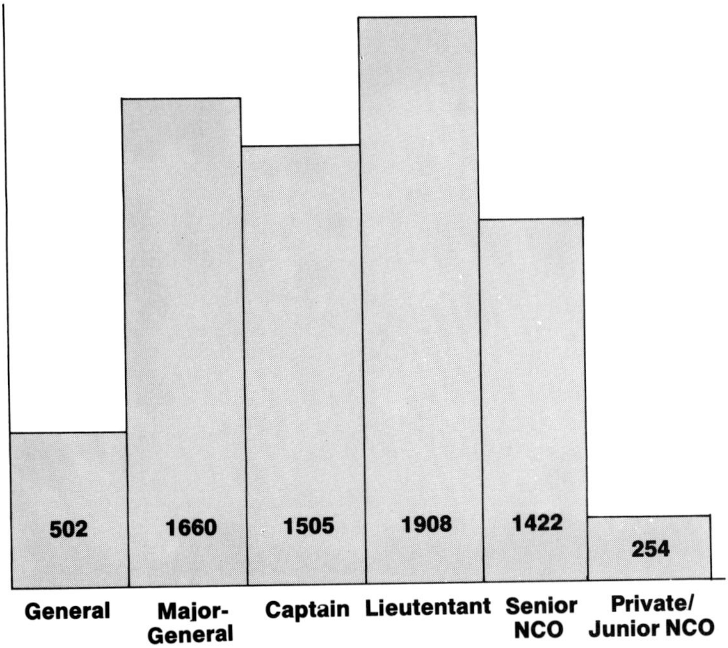

Above
Distribution of the Knight's Cross by rank. The vast majority are well distributed between the ranks of Unterfeldwebel and Oberst.

Opposite above
Distribution by year of the higher awards, from Oakleaves up to and including the Diamonds. As the fighting reached its fiercest and most desperate, so the number of awards increased.

Typical example of a Second Class Iron Cross converted to a Knight's Cross for wearing in action.

available to the British authorities, but rather used a range of grades for a single decoration, the Iron Cross. It should also be noted that the Iron Cross and Knight's Cross were democratically awarded decorations, and, indeed, the Iron Cross was one of the first ever such awards, where no special distinction was made between officer and enlisted ranks. Consider the following figures for British awards:

	World War One	*World War Two*
Victoria Cross	633	182
Military Cross	40,236	10,892
Military Medal	121,454	16,391
Distinguished Flying Cross	572	21,946
Distinguished Flying Medal	-	6,698
Distinguished Service Cross	1,694	4,602
Distinguished Service Medal	5,588	7,290
Distinguished Service Order	9,767	5,444
Distinguished Conduct Medal	25,072	1,898
Air Force Cross	-	1,712
Air Force Medal	-	259
Totals	205,016	77,314

If we compare the World War Two award figures with those for the Iron Cross, certainly the Second and First Classes would appear to have been liberally awarded, but the Knight's Cross award figures compare very favourably with British Gallantry Awards. If we consider that the 'Diamonds' is the highest German gallantry award, then it seems to have been awarded far more sparingly than the Victoria Cross, which was also awarded without distinction of rank in these periods.

It should also be noted that the Knight's Cross series of decorations could be awarded for meritorious service as well as for acts of gallantry. For example, a soldier who is responsible for a single act of great gallantry might receive the Knight's Cross, much as a British soldier might win the Victoria Cross. However, an airman who had flown a particularly high number of combat missions over a long period might also receive the Knight's Cross for long meritorious service, whereas his British counterpart might receive the Distinguished Flying Cross. It can be seen that direct comparisons between British and German decorations can only be partly valid. The Iron Cross should be considered as a decoration in its own right, and not continually compared with other awards.

One further myth about the higher grade Iron Cross awards is that they were awarded more to higher ranks than enlisted men. This is totally untrue. The following chart showing the distribution of Knight's Crosses by rank shows that the highest ranking section, the Generals, received only a small proportion, 6.9 per cent of the awards. Awards of the Knight's Cross were in fact, well distributed throughout the ranks.

	Army	*Navy*	*Waffen-SS*	*Luftwaffe*	*Total*
Generalmajor to Feldmarschall	400	23	17	62	502
Major to Oberst	1216	95	150	199	1660
Hauptmann	932	118	83	372	1505
Leutnant to Oberleutnant	1044	71	99	694	1908
Unteroffizier to Stabsfeldwebel	961	13	75	373	1422
Grenadier to Stabsgefreiter	223	1	14	16	254

A small number of awards of the Knight's Cross of the Iron Cross were made to soldiers in the armies of Germany's allies, as distinct from foreign volounteers serving in the German forces. The total was forty-two, seventeen to Rumania, nine to Italy, eight to Hungary, and two each to Finland, Japan, Slovakia and Spain.

Three Rumanian officers were decorated with the Oakleaves, and there were two Japanese, one Finnish, one Hungarian and one Spanish recipients. Only one award was ever made of the Swords to a foreign officer, included in a posthumous award of the Knight's Cross, Oakleaves, and Swords all made on the same date, 27 May 1943, to Grand Admiral Isoroku Yamamoto of the Imperial Japanese Navy.

KNIGHT'S CROSS RECIPIENTS

SS-Sturmbannführer Heinrich Springer Born in Kiel on 3 November 1914, Heinrich Springer joined the SS-Verfügungstruppe in November 1937, serving in the SS-Standarten 'Germania' and 'Der Führer' and taking part in the annexation of Austria and the occupation of the Sudetenland. In November 1938, he started an Officer Training course at the SS-Junkerschule at Bad Tölz in Bavaria, which lasted until October 1939.

Commissioned into the elite Leibstandarte-SS 'Adolf Hitler' as an SS-Untersturmführer, he served as a platoon leader during the French Campaign, winning the Iron Cross Second Class during the attack on Dunkirk. Promoted to SS-Obersturmführer in September 1940, he served

Heinrich Springer as an SS-Standartenoberjunker photographed at Bad Tölz Officer Training School in 1939, before he was commissioned into the elite Leibstandarte SS 'Adolf Hitler'.

Heinrich Springer (third from right) about to be awarded the Infantry Assault Badge in Bronze, France, 1940.

Below
The advance of the Leibstandarte on Dunkirk, where Springer won the Iron Cross Second Class.

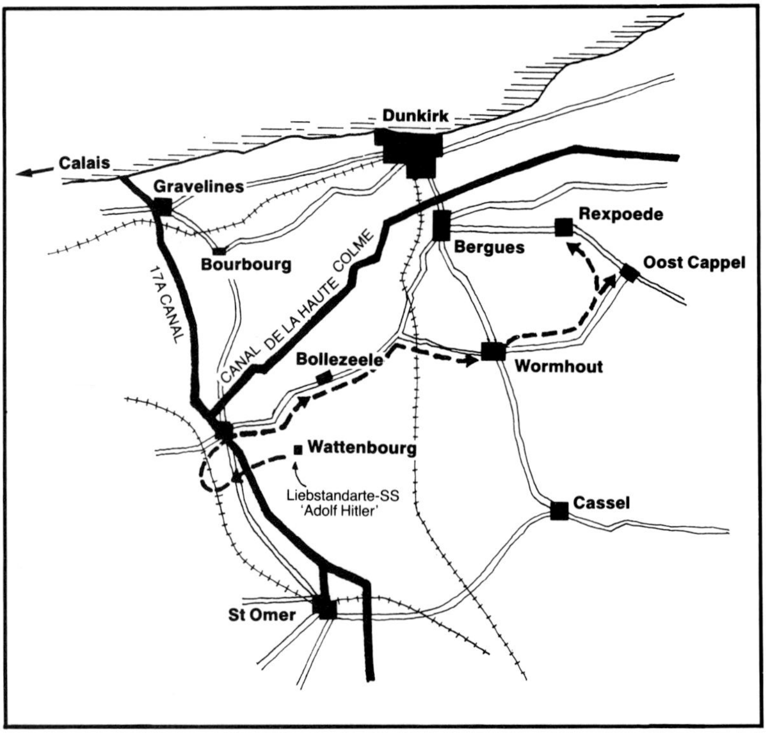

in both the Greek and Yugoslavian Campaigns prior to the attack on Soviet Russia.

During July 1941, as Adjutant to 1 Battalion of the Leibstandarte, Springer led a successful patrol deep behind enemy lines to establish contact with the isolated III Army Corps under General von Mackensen. On returning to his own lines, his patrol was once again sent out, to advise III Army Corps of plans for a link up. Once again this was achieved with total success and no casualties. For this he was awarded the Iron Cross First Class by the Leibstandarte's colourful commander, Josef 'Sepp' Dietrich.

During the attack on Rostov on 20 November 1941, Springer, now an SS-Hauptsturmführer, was leading 3 Coy of the Leibstandarte. His unit attacked the bridge over the Don, and despite furious Russian counter attacks, held on until reinforcements could arrive and consolidate this important victory. On the next day he was wounded during house to house fighting in Rostov and evacuated to a military hospital. Whilst still recovering, he learned that he had been awarded the Knight's Cross of the

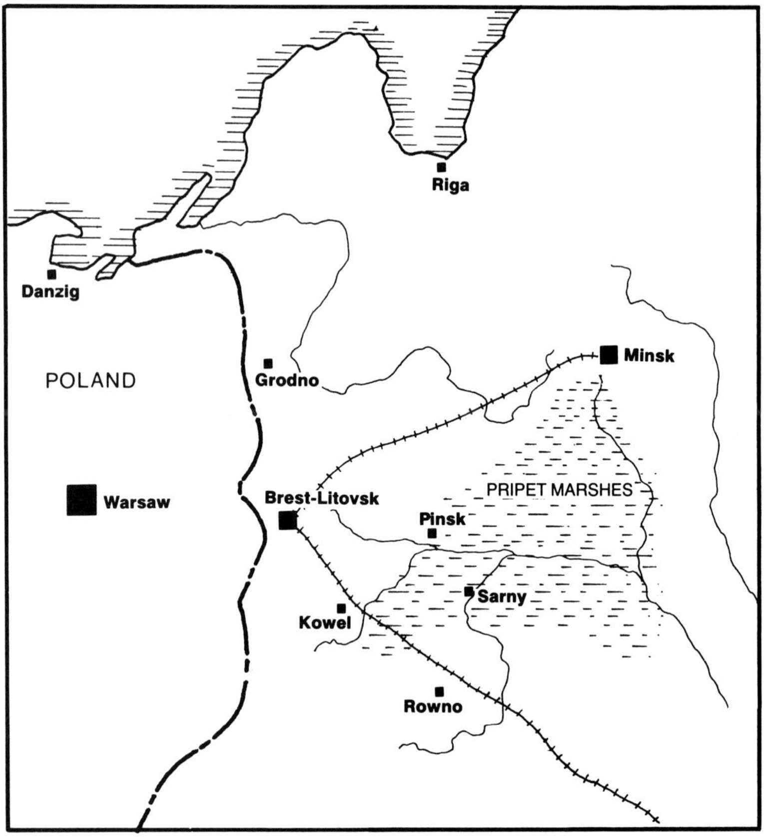

The Pripet Marshes, scene of Spinger's Iron Cross winning patrol. The action took place just east of Rowno.

Opposite above
A rare photograph of the standard of the Leibstandarte being paraded in Metz in 1940. The left escort is SS-Obersturmführer Heinrich Springer. Note the ribbon of the Iron Cross in the buttonhole.

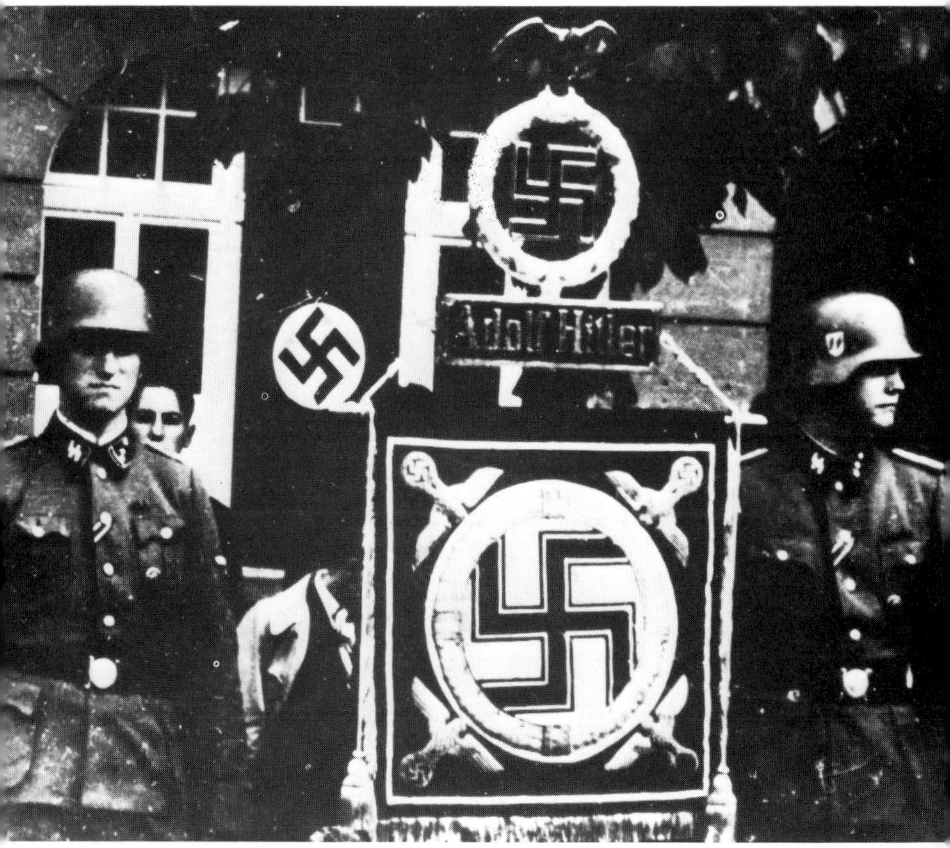

Iron Cross for his capture of the Don bridge. The citation was presented to him personally by Sepp Dietrich at the express wishes of Hitler.

On recovery from his wounds, Springer returned to his unit, and was given command of 1 Coy, which he commanded until he was severely wounded by an exploding tank shell during the fighting for Kharkov in March 1943. Whilst convalescing, he was promoted to SS-Sturmbannführer and assigned to the staff of the newly formed 12 SS-Panzer Division 'Hitler Jugend', as the Divisional Adjutant, in October 1943. Springer's final posting during World War Two was as first ordnance officer on the staff of Generalfeldmarschall Walter Model, Commander of Army Group 'B' on the Western Front. With Model's staff, Springer saw action at Arnhem and in the Ardennes Offensive.

Throughout his military career, Heinrich Springer enjoyed the confidence of his superiors, and the loyalty and respect of his subordinates.

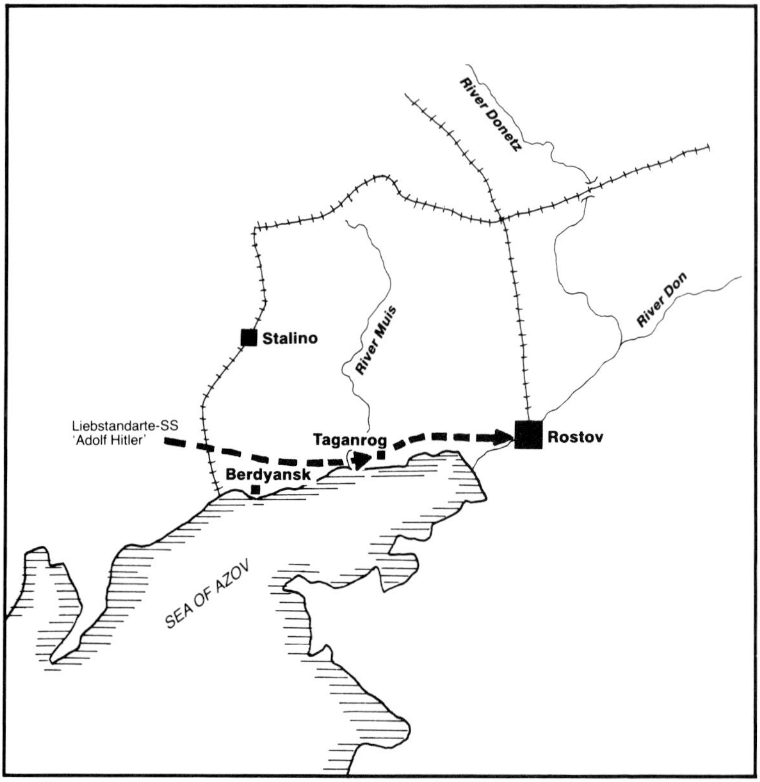

The march of the Leibstandarte on Rostov, where Springer captured the Soviet-held bridge over the Don, winning the Knight's Cross.

Opposite
Russia, June 1942, and Springer poses with another of the Leibstandarte's Knight's Cross winners, Gerd Bremer, at Divisional HQ.

Right
Springer as SS-Hauptsturmführer on the day of the award of his Knight's Cross of the Iron Cross.

His files contained numerous complimentary appraisals from his superiors. As well as his military abilities, Springer's personal bravery in action is well attested to by his numerous decorations. His impressive list of awards includes both Second and First Class Iron Crosses, the Knight's Cross, the Wound Badge in Gold, the East Front Medal, and the Infantry Assault Badge in Bronze. In addition to his German decorations, he was also decorated by Bulgaria and Rumania.

Heinrich Springer lives today in retirement in his native Schleswig-Holstein.

Opposite
Western Front, 1944, and Springer is First Ordnance Officer on the Staff of Generalfeldmarschall Model, with whom he is photographed here.

Right
Springer at the time of his promotion to SS-Sturmbannführer in 1943.

Below
Hauptmann Rudolf Sigmund. A successful night fighter pilot with 28 victories to his credit, Sigmund was accidentally shot down by his own Flak and killed on 3 October 1943.

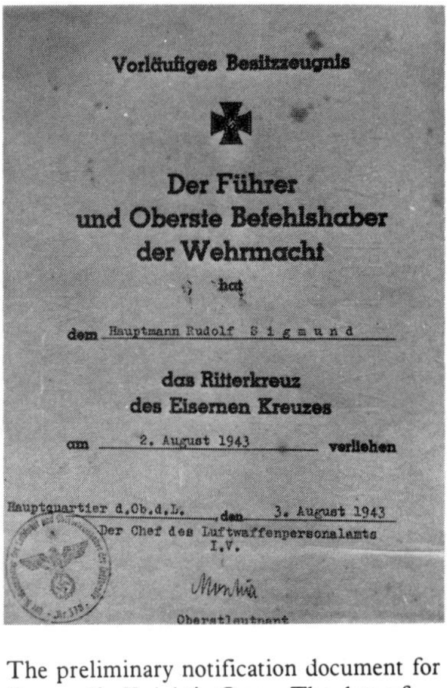

Vorläufiges Besitzzeugnis

Der Führer
und Oberste Befehlshaber
der Wehrmacht

hat

dem Hauptmann Rudolf Sigmund

das Ritterkreuz
des Eisernen Kreuzes

am 2. August 1943 verliehen

Hauptquartier d.Ob.d.L., den 3. August 1943

Der Chef des Luftwaffenpersonalamts
I.V.

Oberstleutnant

The preliminary notification document for Sigmund's Knight's Cross. The date of the award is 2 August 1943.

[illegible] im Luftkampf für seine deutsche Heimat unser lieber Sohn, Bruder u. Neffe, mein geliebter Bräutigam, unser Schwiegersohn und Schwager

der Hauptmann der Luftwaffe

Rudolf Sigmund

Gruppenkommandeur in einem Jagdgeschwader

Träger des Ritterkreuzes, des Deutschen Kreuzes in Gold, der Goldenen Frontflugspange, der Eisernen Kreuze beider Klassen und des Verwundetenabzeichens

Sein menschliches Vorbild an Tapferkeit und Herzensgüte steht vor uns als Verpflichtung für alle Zeit.

In tiefer, stolzer Trauer: Luise Sigmund Wtw., geb. Brauch; Line Sigmund; Rosemarie Elwert; Dr. med. J. Elwert und Frau; Julius Elwert, Fahnenj.-Uffz.; Familien Sigmund, Weisbach; Fam. Brauch.

Reichenbuch, Neckargerach, den 7. Oktober 1943.

Allen denen, die unseres teuren Gefallenen mit so großer Liebe und wohltuender Anteilnahme gedacht haben, bitten wir, nur auf diesem Wege unseren herzlichsten Dank sagen zu dürfen.

Neckargerach, 11. Oktober 1943.

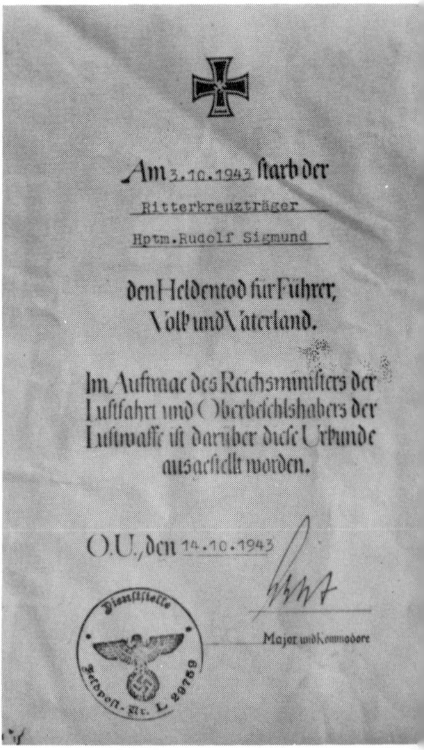

Am 3.10.1943 starb der

Ritterkreuzträger

Hptm. Rudolf Sigmund

den Heldentod für Führer, Volk und Vaterland.

Im Auftrage des Reichsministers der Luftfahrt und Oberbefehlshabers der Luftwaffe ist darüber diese Urkunde ausgestellt worden.

O.U., den 14.10.1943

Major und Kommodore

Dienststelle Feldpost-Nr. L 29759

Opposite
Hauptmann Sigmund's Knight's Cross. Elastic and hook and eye fittings are used in place of the more formal ribbon ties.

Opposite below left
Sigmund's newspaper obituary, listing all of his decorations.

Opposite below right
Certificate notifying the 'Hero's Death' of Hauptmann Sigmund. Note the basic similarity between this and the actual award notification.

SS-Sturmbannführer Leon Degrelle, commander of 28 SS-Sturmbrigade 'Wallonien'. Degrelle reached the rank of SS-Standartenführer and went on to win the Oakleaves to his Knight's Cross.

Opposite
Knight's Cross holder Generaladmiral Alfred Saalwachter, commander-in-chief of Marine Gruppen Kommando West. Saalwachter died in Russian captivity.

Right
SS-Hauptsturmführer Fritz Klingenberg, commander of 2 Kradschutzbataillon of SS-Panzer Division 'Das Reich'. Klingenberg received his Knight's Cross in 1941 during the Jugoslavian Campaign. He was killed in action in March 1945.

Below
Two Knight's Cross winners from Panzergrenadier Division 'Grossdeutschland', Oberwachtmeister Wilhelm Wegner, left, and Oberfeldwebel Martin Beilig, right.

Opposite
Leutnant Adolf Schmhl, who was decorated with the Knight's Cross on 7 July 1942 whilst serving with 6 Infanterie Regiment on the Russian Front.

Right
Oberwachtmeister Wilhelm Kessel of the elite 'Grossdeutschland' Division. Kessel won his Knight's Cross in February 1944. Note the Second Class ribbon on the lapel.

Oberfeldwebel Wriedt of 138 Gebirsjäger Regiment. Strangely, no ribbon for the Second Class is being worn. Walter Wriedt won his Knight's Cross in October 1943.

Right
Oberst Hans Jordan, commander of 49 Infantry Regiment. Oberst Jordan later won the Oakleaves and was elevated to the rank of General der Infanterie.

Leutnant Otto Engel of Kampfgeschwader 53 'Legion Kondor'. Awarded the Knight's Cross on 28 February 1945, Engel also held the Bomber Flight Clasp for 500 combat missions, and the German Cross in Gold.

SS-Unterscharführer Remi Schrijnen of SS-Sturmbrigade 'Langemarck'. At the time of winning his award, Remi Schrijnen held the rank of SS-Sturmann, and is one of only a handful of Belgians to have won the coveted Knight's Cross.

Opposite
Major Ernst Thomsen. Originally a naval pilot officer on the pocket battleship *Admiral Graf Spee,* Thomsen served with Kampfgeschwader 26 on anti-shipping strikes. He was awarded the Knight's Cross on 24 October 1944. Major Thomsen joined the West German Navy after the war as a jet fighter pilot and retired as a Kapitän zur See.

Knight's Cross of the Iron Cross with Oakleaves.

Opposite
Korvettenkapitän Heinrich Bleichrodt, centre, commander of *U-48* and *U-109* and winner of the Knight's Cross with Oakleaves.

Left
Reverse of the Knight's Cross with Oakleaves. Silver content marks appear on the rim of the Knight's Cross and the lower right reverse of the Oakleaves.

THE OAKLEAVES

The first 'addition' to the Knight's Cross award, the Oakleaves were instituted on 3 June 1940. The award consists of a small silver cluster of three oakleaves, with the central leaf overlapping the lower two. The clasp was struck in solid silver and had a smooth slightly concave reverse onto which was welded a suspension loop. On the original award piece, the silver content mark is usually stamped on the left hand side of the reverse, with the maker's mark occasionally stamped on the right hand side. Privately purchased additional awards could be obtained through retail outlets and can be found in a variety of materials from silver plated brass to very high grade solid silver.

The clasp measures 20 by 20mm and was normally issued in a small black case lined with white satin to the lid and black velvet to the base.

A total of 890 awards were made, the first being to Generalleutnant Eduard Dietl on 19 July 1940 for his successful command of the German forces at Narvik. With the award came promotion to General der Gebirgstruppe.

OAKLEAVES RECIPIENTS

Korvettenkapitän Heinrich Bleichrodt Heinrich Bleichrodt was born in 1909 and joined the Reichsmarine in 1926 serving on a variety of vessels including the cruiser *Karlsruhe,* the old battleship *Schleswig Holstein,* the sail trainer *Gorch Fock* and the heavy cruiser *Admiral Hipper.*

Shortly after the war's start he began training as a U-Boat officer. After training, he was assigned to *U-8* before being given his own command, *U-48,* in August 1940. He was so successful that only two months later on 24 October, he was awarded the Knights Cross. His next command was

Heinrich 'Ajax' Bleichrodt, commander of *U-109*.

U-67, then *U-109* as part of 2 U-Flotille. As commander of *U-109,* with the rank of Kapitänleutnant, Bleichrodt received the Oakleaves on 23 September 1942.

As with many experienced U-Boat officers, Bleichrodt was transferred to a training establishment where his experience would be put to good use instructing future U-Boat commanders. His final credit stood at thirty enemy vessels destroyed, plus one destroyer, totalling over 203,000 tons.

As well as being a brave and resourceful commander, Bleichrodt had a sharp wit. In Wilhelmshaven, after the war's end, Bleichrodt was ordered by a British admiral to remove his Knight's Cross because of the swastika. Bleichrodt merely turned his Knights Cross back to front, so that the plain reverse was shown. When the British admiral objected once again the next day, Bleichrodt, a Prussian, pointed to the institution date of 1813, and reminded the admiral that it was the arrival of the Prussians at Waterloo which had saved the day for Wellington. Surely the British admiral could not object to that!

Oberleutnant Ekkehard Kylling-Schmidt of Grenadier Regiment 587. He won the Oakleaves on 4 December 1942 having previously won the Knight's Cross on 20 October 1941 as a Leutnant in 26 Infanterie Regiment.

Major Helmut Wick of Jagdgeschwader 2 'Richthofen'. Wick was the fourth recipient of the Oakleaves. He died in action in November 1940 over the Isle of Wight, shot down by Flying Officer John Dundas. He had scored 56 victories.

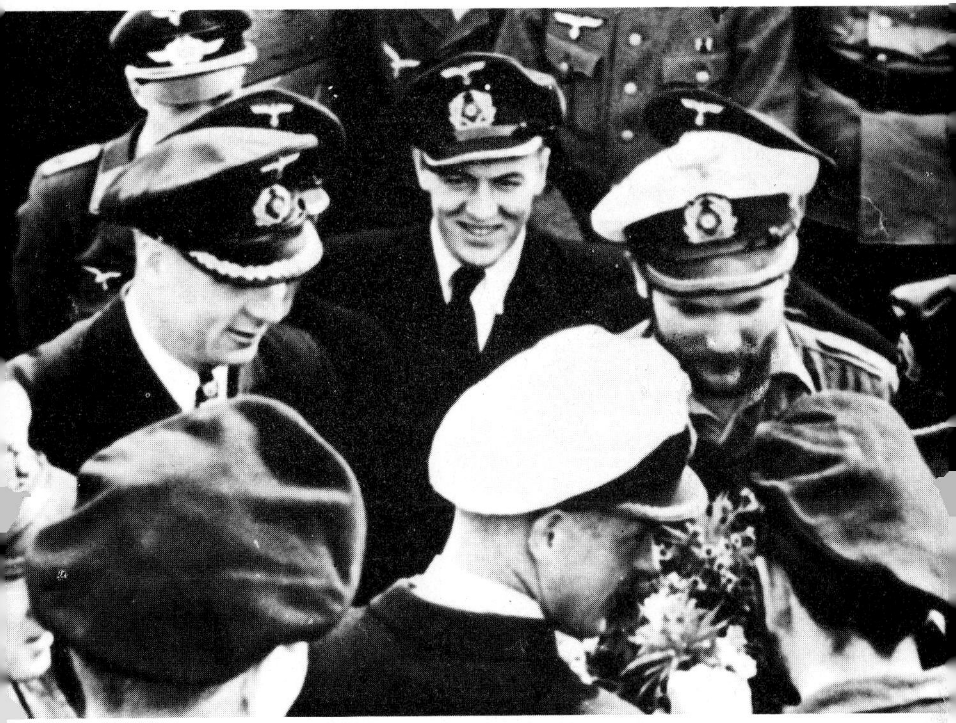

U-377's last commander, Oberleutnant Gerhard Kluth in the traditional white top cap of a U-Boat captain. Left of centre is Oakleaves winner Heinrich Lehmann-Willenbrock, the flotilla commander.

Opposite
SS-Hauptsturmführer Heinz Macher of 16 Pioniere Kompanie of SS-Panzer Regiment 3 'Deutschland'. As well as the Knight's Cross with Oakleaves, Macher won the German Cross in Gold, the Close Combat Clasp and the award for single-handed destruction of an enemy tank.

Right
SS-Standartenführer Johannes Mühlenkamp commander of 5 SS-Panzer Division 'Wiking', one of the best of the Waffen-SS Divisions, with an excellent combat record. Mühlenkamp survived the war and now lives in retirement.

THE SWORDS AND OAKLEAVES

Instituted on 15 July 1941, the Swords and Oakleaves award consists of the basic Oakleaves award, but with the addition of a pair of crossed swords at the base. The crossed swords measure 24mm in length, and are crossed at an angle of 40 degrees, giving the clasp an overall size of 25 by 10mm. The average weight of the award piece is 7.8g. The award came in a case similar to that used for the Oakleaves.

Two distinct types are known. The actual award piece was in genuine silver and normally carries both the silver content mark and the makers mark on the reverse. Its main identifying feature however, is that the swords at the base are detailed on both obverse and reverse faces, and have a gap between the crosspiece and the opposing blade. The second type normally encountered is the privately purchased jeweller copy. This differs in having a plain reverse to the swords, and has the crosspieces touching the opposing blades.

Examination of many contemporary photographs will show several apparent variants. This can be explained by the practice often encountered of units presenting popular recipients of the Swords with hand made

Opposite
Freggattenkapitän Lehmann Willenbrock, commander of 9 U-Flotilla awaits an incoming U-Boat. He had won both the Knight's Cross and the Oakleaves as commander of *U-96.* He ended the war with a total score of 205,000 tons to his credit.

Above right
Close-up of the Swords and Oakleaves to the Knight's Cross of the Iron Cross.

Right
Reverse view of the Swords and Oakleaves Clasp. This is the jeweller's copy type. Note the plain undetailed reverse to the Swords. The '800' silver mark is clearly seen.

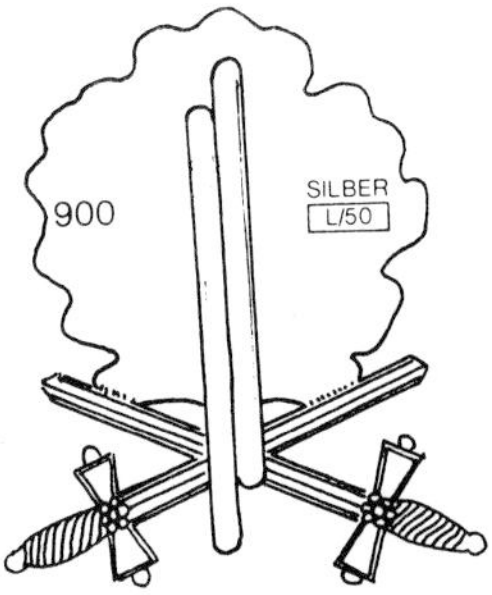

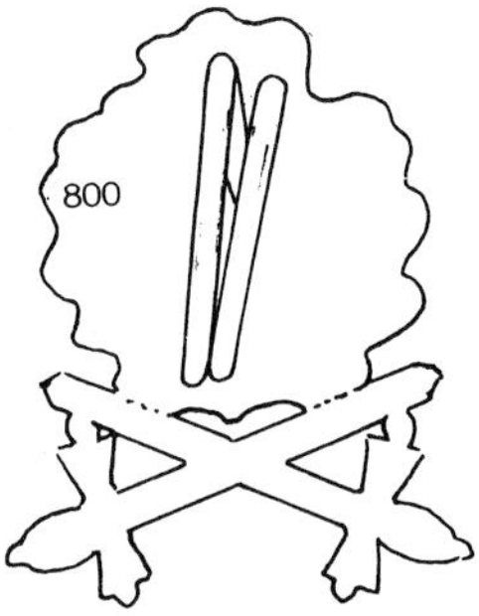

Details of typical reverse views of official issue, left, and jeweller's copy, right, Swords and Oakleaves.

A rare and unusual variant of the Swords and Oakleaves Clasp with much larger Swords than normal. This piece has no silver content mark.

Opposite
Korvettenkapitän Otto Kretschmer, probably Germany's greatest U-Boat ace in World War Two.

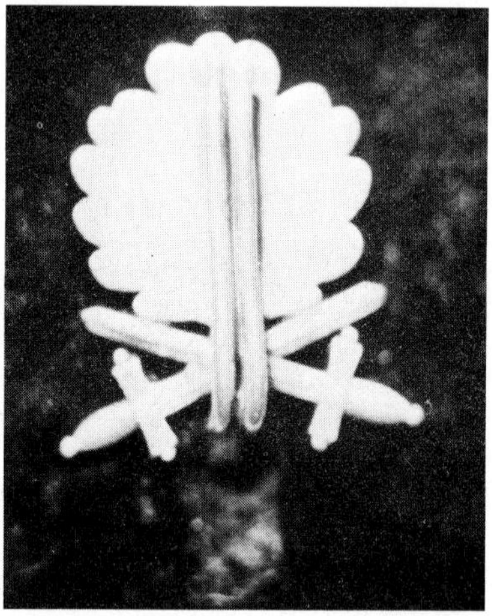

Reverse of the standard Swords and Oakleaves. Note the detailing to the reverse of the Swords.

copies before the official award was made. Many recipients continued to wear these copies out of affection for their comrades.

A total of 159 awards of the Swords were made. The first was awarded to Oberstleutnant Adolf Galland on 21 June 1941 after his victory score had reached sixty-nine. The final recipient was Oberstleutnant Josef Bremm, Commander of 990 Grenadier Regiment. This last award was approved by Grossadmiral Dönitz on 9 May 1945.

SWORDS AND OAKLEAVES RECIPIENTS

Korvettenkapitän Otto Kretschmer Born on 1 May 1912, Otto Kretschmer scored his first victory as commander of *U-23* when, in October 1939, he sank the small coaster *Glen Farg*. His first few months of wartime activity, however, were taken up principally by minelaying operations in British waters, and patrolling off the Orkney and Shetland

Opposite
Grossadmiral Karl Dönitz, Commander-in-Chief of the German Navy. Although, his U-Boats sank an incredible 14 million tons of allied shipping, Dönitz would regard his greatest success as the saving of nearly two million refugees from Russian captivity in the closing weeks of the war.

Freggattenkapitän Erich Topp, commander of *U-552*, was awarded the Swords on 17 August 1942. He accounted for over 243,000 tons of Allied shipping. After the war he served with the West German Navy, reaching the rank of Rear Admiral.

Isles. His successful command of *U-23* on these operations brought him the award of the Iron Crosses Second and First Class.

In April 1940, Kretschmer was given command of a new craft, *U-99*, assuming actual command of her on 1 May, his twenty-eight birthday. His expertise in command of *U-99* was to make him the most successful U-Boat commander of World War Two. On 4 August 1940, only three months after being given command of his new vessel, Kretschmer was presented with the Knight's Cross in recognition of having sunk 117,000 tons of allied shipping.

Within a further three months, Kapitänleutnant Kretschmer had increased his total to 200,000 tons, and was rewarded for this score with the Oakleaves to his Knight's Cross on 4 November. He was the sixth recipient of this award.

Kretschmer's luck could not hold out for ever, and, on 17 March 1941, his U-Boat was attacked and sunk by the British destroyer HMS *Walker*. Luckily though, Kretschmer and most of his crew were saved. At the time of his capture, Korvettenkapitän Kretschmer had sunk a total of 266,629 tons of allied shipping, representing forty-four ships.

Kretschmer was eventually sent to Bowmanville prisoner of war camp in Canada, and learned in captivity that he had been awarded the Swords on 26 December 1941, only the fifth recipient of this coveted award, and one of only five Kriegsmarine personnel to win it.

Kretschmer ended the war with the rank of Fregattenkapitän and after a

period at Kiel University where he studied maritime law, he returned to the service he loved, and at the time of his retirement he held the rank of Flotillenadmiral with the West German Navy.

Fregattenkapitän Reinhard Sühren Born in Langenschwalbach in 1916 into a military family. He entered Naval service in 1935 and was first officer of the Watch on *U-48* when the signal arrived notifying the award of a Ritterkreuz. The commander, Heinrich Bleichrodt, was unsure as to whether the award was for him or for Sühren. Many of *U-48*'s successes were night attacks when Sühren had command, and gave the fire orders. Bleichrodt queried the award but Dönitz was adamant that only U-Boat commanders should receive the Knight's Cross, despite Bleichrodt's arguments.

Bleichrodt had obviously struck home, however, and Sühren was awarded the Knight's Cross on 3 November 1940, the first ever award of the Knight's Cross to a U-Boat first officer. This was followed the next year by the Oakleaves, by which time he had his own command, *U-564*. The award was made on 31 December 1941. Sühren eventually added the Swords to his Oakleaves on 1 September 1942 as the eighteenth recipient of this award. His final score was in excess of 261,000 tons.

Sühren ended the war as commanding officer of the U-Boat Fleet Norway-North Sea.

Awarded the Swords on 15 July 1941, Oberst Walter Oesau was killed in action against American fighters in May 1944. He had reached a score of 128 enemy aircraft destroyed. He was one of the few recipients of the Spanish Cross with diamonds, and flew with JG 51 and JG 53.

Opposite
SS-Obersturmbannführer Otto Weidinger. Weidinger's Swords and Oakleaves can be seen clearly in this photograph as can the Infantry Close Combat Clasp.

SS-Obersturmbannführer Otto Weidinger Born in Aalen on 27 May 1914, Otto Weidinger joined the SS-Verfügungstruppe in 1934 and graduated from the SS-Junkerschule Braunschweig in 1935. At the outbreak of war in 1939, Weidinger served in the Aufklärungsabteilung of SS-Standarte 'Deutschland', part of the SS-Verfügungsdivision. He won the Iron Cross Second Class on 15 November 1939 during the Polish

campaign. Weidinger's Aufklärungsabteilung saw further action during the French campaign and Weidinger was decorated with the Iron Cross First Class on 25 July 1940.

After taking part in the Yugoslavian campaign and the opening phases of the attack on the Soviet Union, Weidinger was appointed as tactical instructor at the SS-Junkerschule where he himself had been trained. He then returned to his Division, now entitled 'Das Reich', and served with distinction as commander of 1 Battalion, 'Deutschland' Regiment. Whilst commanding this unit on the Russian Front, Weidinger was decorated with the German Cross in Gold on 26 November 1943. Promoted to command 4 SS-Panzer Grenadier Regiment 'Der Führer', Weidinger, now an SS-Sturmbannführer, was awarded the Knights Cross on 21 April 1944 for distinguished service on the Russian Front.

Units of 2 SS-Panzer Grenadier Division 'Das Reich' were sent to France during late 1943 and early 1944 for regrading as a full Panzer Division. The Division served during the battle for the Falaise Gap, and Weidinger was decorated with the Oakleaves to his Knight's Cross for bravery and leadership during these actions. The award was made on 26 December 1944.

After the ill-fated Ardennes action, 'Das Reich' was hastily refitted and sent to Hungary where it fought a desperate rearguard action through Czechoslovakia and into Austria. For his gallantry during these hectic days Weidinger received the Swords on 6 May 1945. He ended the war with the rank of SS-Obersturmbannführer, and after his retirement, wrote the definitive history of his unit, entitled *Division Das Reich.*

SS-Brigadeführer und Generalmajor Der Waffen-SS Kurt Meyer

Born in Jerxheim on 23 December 1910, Kurt Meyer served as a Police Officer before joining the Leibstandarte in 1934. By the outbreak of war he had reached the rank of SS-Hauptsturmführer. During the Polish Campaign, Meyer won the Iron Cross Second Class and subsequently won the First Class, on 8 June 1940, during the French Campaign.

It was during the Greek campaign however, that Meyer's real flair and bravery came to the fore. As an SS-Sturmbannführer in command of the Aufklärungsabteilung of the Leibstandarte, Meyer's brilliant and dashing leadership was responsible for the capture of the Klissura Pass. After the Leibstandarte's attack had bogged down, Meyer had spurred on his men and personally led them into the attack. For his gallantry, he was awarded the Knight's Cross on 18 May 1941.

Meyer's fame and popularity with his men grew rapidly, and on 23 May 1943 his continued success and personal bravery brought him the Oakleaves to his Knight's Cross, after the battle of Kharkov. At this time, Meyer held the rank of SS-Obersturmbannführer.

SS-Obersturmbannführer Kurt 'Panzer' Meyer. A veteran of the Leibstandarte, Meyer was given command of 12 SS-Panzer Division 'Hitlerjugend' and attained the rank of Generalmajor at the age of only 33.

Following the formation of the 12 SS-Panzer Division 'Hitlerjugend' in 1943, a cadre of experienced soldiers was transferred from the Leibstandarte to form the core of the new unit. Meyer was given command of one of its Regiments, 25 SS-Panzer Grenadier Regiment.

Meyer's steadfastness during the defensive battles in Normandy in 1944 did not go unrewarded, and on the death of the divisional commander, Fritz Witt, Meyer was given command of the Division, with the rank of SS-Oberführer. One of the youngest senior officers of the Waffen-SS, Meyer was decorated with the Swords in recognition of his achievements during the Normandy battles. The award was made on 27 August 1944, but only eleven days later he was captured by Belgian partisans. He was subsequently held as a prisoner of war in England until the war's end.

After the war, Meyer was brought before an Allied Military Tribunal and tried for crimes allegedly committed by his unit during the bitter fighting for Caen. Meyer's divisional personnel consisted to a large degree of very young men and, whilst they were fanatically brave and dedicated, allegations of the execution of prisoners were made against them, damaging the reputation of the Division. Meyer was sentenced to death. As divisional commander he had to take responsibility for the actions of his men. Following a wave of protests, however, this sentence was commuted and he was released in 1954 after almost ten years imprisonment.

His health failing, Meyer died of a heart attack on his fiftieth birthday on 23 December 1960. His funeral was attended by thousands of his former wartime comrades.

Whatever the validity or otherwise of crimes alleged to have been carried out by his men, there can be no doubting Meyer's personal gallantry which made him a worthy winner of the Swords.

THE SWORDS, OAKLEAVES AND DIAMONDS

The Diamonds were instituted on 15 July 1941, though in fact the official order was not published until 28 September. They consist of a hand crafted set of silver swords and oakleaves, set with small diamonds. The clasp was usually made in 935 grade silver and is hollow backed rather than die-struck, to allow for better reflection of the stones. Due to the fact that these awards were hand crafted, no two are exactly identical and the precise number of stones and their placement may vary. Generally speaking the total weight of diamonds came to around 2.7 carats. The award's overall weight is around 18 grams.

A number of jeweller's copies were manufactured for the winners of the Diamonds or Brillantenträger, as few wished to risk losing the formal decoration by wearing it in action. These copies vary considerably from

An original award piece of the Knight's Cross with Oakleaves Swords and Diamonds. Note the more elongated, oval shape of the oakleaves as compared to the standard Oakleaves Clasp.

Contemporary jeweller's copy of the Oakleaves, Swords and Diamonds based on the Standard Swords and Oakleaves. Note that this piece has stones in the Sword hilts.

manufacturer to manufacturer. The best copies are those based on the standard Swords and Oakleaves clasp already described, but set with small stones. Copies based on the jeweller copies of the Swords and Oakleaves are also known. Both of these types may be found with or without the inclusion of stones on the sword hilts as well as the Oakleaves.

The Swords, Oakleaves and Diamonds were awarded in a small black case measuring 107 by 82 by 32mm, lined with black velvet to the base and white satin to the lid.

Only twenty-seven awards of the Swords, Oakleaves and Diamonds were made. Each recipient's career is covered in the following pages in the chronological order in which the award was made to him. The orders in which he had received the Oakleaves and the Diamonds are indicated by figures in parenthesis after these awards.

THE SWORDS, OAKLEAVES AND DIAMONDS RECIPIENTS — THE BRILLANTENTRÄGER

1. **Oberst Werner Mölders** Werner Mölders was awarded the Knight's

Cross on 29 May 1940, the Oakleaves (2) on 21 September 1940 and the Swords (2) on 22 June 1941. As the commanding officer of JG 51, he received the Diamonds on 16 July 1941, after reaching a score of one hundred aerial victories, the last twenty-eight of which were achieved in only twenty-four days. With the award came promotion to General der Jagdflieger, at the age of only twenty-seven. Mölders career would no doubt have brought him further honours, but he was tragically killed in an air crash only a few months after the award of the Diamonds. This popular figure was given a state funeral as befitted a national hero, and he was buried in the Invaliden cemetery in Berlin, near to Germany's great fighter pilot of World War One, Baron von Richthofen.

2. **Generalleutnant Adolf Galland** Adolf Galland was awarded the Knight's Cross on 1 August 1940, the Oakleaves (3) on 24 September 1940, and the Swords (1) on 21 June 1941.

Born in 1912, Adolf Galland was a close friend and colleague of Werner Mölders and their careers were closely paralleled until Mölders untimely death. Galland, like Mölders, served with distinction during the Spanish Civil War and was in fact one of only twenty eight recipients of the Spanish Cross with Diamonds.

Galland was awarded the Knight's Cross of the Iron Cross after scoring his seventeenth victory. Galland, at this time ranked as major, went on to increase his score to forty, at which point he became the third recipient of the Oakleaves. At this time he was commander of JG 26 'Schlageter'.

Active in the ferocious air battles with the Royal Air Force over the English Channel, Galland's skill soon brought his score up to sixty-nine, and with it the award of the coveted Swords, a special honour as he was the first ever recipient, beating his great friend Mölders by just one day. Galland still commanded JG 26, but now with the rank of Oberstleutnant.

Success continued for Galland, and, on reaching his ninety-fourth victory he was awarded his country's ultimate decoration, the Diamonds on 28 January 1942. This time, however, it was he who was beaten by his friend Mölders to the honour of being the first recipient.

Galland's score continued to grow, until his final score of one hundred and four was reached. Although this score is by no means the highest attained by a Luftwaffe pilot, it must be remembered that Galland scored his victories mainly on the Western front against skilled RAF pilots. Many of the exceptionally high scores reached by other pilots were against Soviet aircraft, often obsolete and initially at least, flown by poorly trained and motivated pilots, and more plentiful. Galland's score therefore justly includes him as one of the great German fighter pilots.

When his friend Mölders died, Galland took his place as Inspector

Adolf Galland, one of Germany's great fighter pilots, who eventually became General of Fighters and one of the first jet pilots. He also wears the Pilot/Observer's badge with Diamonds on the left breast pocket.

General of Fighters, with the rank of Generalleutnant. He was instrumental in the formation of the Luftwaffe's jet fighter units in the closing stages of the war. He openly disagreed with many of Hitler's and Göring's plans for the use of the Luftwaffe's precious fighters. Generalleutnant Galland survived the war. He had earned the deep respect of friend and foe alike.

A successful businessman after the war, Galland is still alive. His biography *Die Ersten und die Letzten* (*The First and the Last*) is a fine record of the rise and fall of the Luftwaffe's fighter arm.

3. **Major Gordon Gollob** Gordon Gollob was awarded the Knight's Cross on 18 September 1941, the Oakleaves (38) on 26 October 1941 and the Swords (13) on 24 June 1942. Major Gollob's award of the Diamonds came on 30 August 1942 following his one hundred and fiftieth victory. He was commanding officer of JG 77. A popular figure, he worked with Generalleutnant Galland on the jet fighter programme, and ended the war with the rank of Oberst, and a score of one hundred and fifty. He is still alive.

4. **Hauptmann Hans-Joachim Marseilles** Marseilles was awarded the Knight's Cross on 22 February 1942, the Oakleaves (97) on 6 June 1942 and the Swords (12) on 18 June 1942. One of Germany's greatest war heroes from the early part of the war, this young ace received his Diamonds on 2 September 1942 shortly after scoring his hundred and twenty-sixth victory, flying with JG 27 in North Africa. This young virtuoso was killed when, on bailing out of a damaged aircraft, he was struck by its tailplane. His final score of one hundred and fifty-eight victories, despite some post war speculation about its accuracy, is all the more impressive when one considers that they were achieved against well trained RAF pilots within the space of little more than one year. Much of Hauptmann Marseilles personal equipment, insignia, etc, is on display at the Luftwaffe Museum at Uetersen, West Germany.

5. **Oberst Hermann Graf** Graf was awarded the Knights Cross on 10 January 1942, and the Oakleaves (93) *and* the Swords (11) on 2 May 1942. After being thus distinguished with the award of both the Oakleaves and the Swords on the same day, Graf, flying with JG 52, went on to win the Diamonds on 16 September 1942 after reaching a score of two hundred victories, the first pilot to do so. He ended the war with a final tally of two hundred and twelve victories, and he is still alive.

6. **Generalfeldmarschall Erwin Rommel** Rommel was awarded the

Knight's Cross on 26 May 1940. He became the tenth recipient of the Oakleaves on 20 March 1941, and the sixth of the Swords on 20 January 1942. He was the first non-Luftwaffe recipient of the Diamonds, which were awarded on 11 March 1943, whilst he was Commander-in-Chief of Army Group 'Afrika'. Following the defeat of the Axis forces in Africa, Rommel was appointed to supervise the defences on the French coast, the much vaunted 'Atlantic Wall'. His name having been linked with the assassination attempt on Hitler, he was forced to commit suicide to avoid the disgrace of a public trial.

Even in post war Germany, where little recognition is given to former soldiers of the Third Reich period, Rommel's name lives on, having been given to a guided missile destroyer of the West German Navy. Werner Mölders and Admiral Gunther Lütjens, of *Bismarck* fame, have been similarly honoured.

7. **Kapitän zur See Wolfgang Lüth** Born in Riga in 1913, Lüth's first successes came whilst commanding *U-138* when he was awarded the Knight's Cross on 24 October 1940 in recognition of having sunk 49,000

U-Boat commander Wolfgang Lüth, in leather coat, chats to his comrade Erich Topp. Lüth was one of only two naval recipients of the Diamonds.

tons of enemy shipping. Lüth held the rank of Oberleutnant zur See at this time. Lüth continued his ravages of allied shipping, winning the Oakleaves (142) on 13 November 1942 as Kapitänleutnant in command of *U-43* after sinking nearly 82,000 tons of shipping. The Swords (29) followed, when he was commander of *U-181,* on 15 April 1943. Lüth's Diamonds were awarded on 9 August 1943 as Korvettenkapitän commanding *U-181.*

By August 1944 it had been decided that Lüth's experience was too valuable to risk losing on further combat postings. By now he had sunk over 250,000 tons of allied shipping, and Germany could not afford to lose men of his calibre. Promoted to Kapitän zur See, Lüth was posted as commander of the Marineschule Murwik where his experience would be put to good use training new personnel.

Lüth remained at his post until just after the war's end, when failing to answer the challenge of a sentry, he was shot dead. It is ironic that a man who had lived with danger for so long, should die accidentally, after the war's end.

8. **Major Walter Nowotny** Flying with JG 54, Nowotny was awarded the Knight's Cross on 14 September 1942, and the Oakleaves (293) on 3 September 1943. Awarded the Swords (37) only days later on 22 September 1943, he was almost as quickly decorated with the Diamonds on 19 October 1943 after scoring his two hundred and fiftieth victory, the first to reach this incredible score. He was also one of the Luftwaffe's first jet fighter pilots, and used his Me 262 jet to great effect on Allied bombers. He was killed on 8 November 1944 almost certainly shot down by P-51 Mustangs of the USAAF near his base.

9. **Generalmajor Adalbert Schulz** Schulz was awarded the Knight's Cross on 29 September 1940, the Oakleaves (47) on 31 December 1941, and the Swords (33) on 6 August 1943. He was decorated with the Diamonds on 14 November 1943 whilst commanding Panzer Regiment 25 on the Eastern Front, with the rank of Oberst. Schulz was promoted to the rank of Generalmajor and given command of the famed 7 Panzer Division. A typical front line fighting officer, Schulz was killed in January 1944 when struck on the head by a shell fragment whilst leading his troops in battle.

10. **Oberst Hans-Ulrich Rudel.** (Details of Rudel's awards are given in the section dealing with the Golden Oakleaves, Swords and Diamonds, which follows this section.)

11. **Generalleutnant Hyazinth Graf Strachwitz** Awarded the Knight's Cross on 25 August 1941, the Oakleaves (144) on 17 November

1942, and the Swords (27) on 28 March 1943, Oberst Strachwitz gained the Diamonds on 15 April 1944 whilst commanding a Panzer Kampfgruppe on the Eastern Front. He had previously served with the elite 'Grossdeutschland' Division. With the Diamonds came promotion to Generalmajor and command of 1 Panzer Division. A brave and popular commander, he ended the war with the rank of Generalleutnant.

12. **SS-Obergruppenführer und General Der Waffen-SS Herbert Otto Gille** A brave and experienced officer, Gille had won both Second and First Class Iron Crosses during World War One. His command of the elite Waffen-SS 'Wiking' Division on the Eastern Front during World War Two brought him deserved success and recognition. The 'Wiking' Division gained a fine fighting reputation and was much feared and respected by the Red Army. This was in no small part due to the leadership of Gille. Gille was awarded the Knight's Cross on 8 October 1942, the Oakleaves (315) on 1 November 1943 and the Swords (47) on 18 February 1944. He received his Diamonds on 19 April 1944 and subsequently commanded the IV SS-Panzer Korps. Gille survived the war and died in 1966 at the age of sixty-nine.

13. **Generaloberst Hans Hube** An immensely popular officer, loved and respected by his men, Hube was a charismatic figure. He had lost an arm during World War One, yet was always to be found in the thick of the fighting in amongst his men. Hube was awarded the Knight's Cross on 1 August 1941, the Oakleaves (62) on 17 January 1942, and the Swords (22) on 21 December 1942. He received the Diamonds on 20 April 1944. At this time he was a General der Panzertruppe, but was promoted to Generaloberst. He died in an air crash the very next day.

14. **Generalfeldmarschall Albert Kesselring** Kesselring was a dynamic personality and a very competent field commander, as evidenced by his defensive actions in Italy when he was Commander-in-Chief South, Monte Cassino being a prime example. His Diamonds were awarded on 19 July 1944, following the award of the Knight's Cross on 30 September 1939, the Oakleaves (78) on 25 February 1942, and the Swords (15) on 18 July 1942. Kesselring survived the war but was put on trial for excesses committed by troops under his command, mainly against partisans. His sentence was commuted due to bad health and he died in retirement at the age of seventy-four in 1960.

15. **Oberstleutnant Helmut Lent** One of the Luftwaffe's greatest night fighter pilots, Lent was awarded the Knight's Cross on 30 August 1941,

the Oakleaves (98) on 6 June 1942, and the Swords (32) on 3 August 1943. He was awarded the Diamonds after scoring his hundred and tenth victory. The award was made on 31 July 1944. Lent was the first night fighter pilot to win the Diamonds. He was the commander of NJG 3. In October 1944, Lent's aircraft was involved in a crash, and he died of his injuries two days later.

16. **SS-Oberstgruppenführer Und Generaloberst Der Waffen-SS Joseph Dietrich** Born in Bavaria in 1892, Dietrich enlisted in an artillery regiment in 1911 and served with some distinction, winning both Second and First Class Iron Crosses during World War One. Before the war's end Dietrich also saw service in the new German tank units, experience which was to stand him in good stead in later years. At the end of the war, Dietrich left the army with the rank of sergeant.

An early admirer of Hitler, Dietrich became his personal bodyguard commander in 1933, and as this bodyguard grew, so Dietrich's fortunes grew also. This bodyguard ultimately became the elite Leibstandarte-SS 'Adolf Hitler'. For his command of this unit during the Polish Campaign, Dietrich won the Bars to both of his 1914 Iron Crosses.

After the close of the Polish Campaign, the Leibstandarte was transferred to the west where it saw tough action against the British Expeditionary Force, acquitting itself well. On 4 July 1940, Dietrich received the Knight's Cross for his command of the Leibstandarte during this period.

'Sepp' Dietrich's charismatic character, and undoubted personal bravery made him a popular figure, much admired by Hitler, and adored by his men. It is scarcely surprising that the Leibstandarte was allowed to expand rapidly under his command, and in every campaign in which it fought fresh honours were won by its officers and men.

On 31 December 1941, Dietrich received the Oakleaves (41) for his command of the Leibstandarte during the invasion of the Balkan countries. Following the invasion of the Soviet Union in 1941, the Leibstandarte was almost constantly in action, invariably where the fighting was at its fiercest. Its losses were tremendous, but its achievements in defence as well as in attack brought the Leibstandarte an almost legendary reputation. On 16 March 1943, Dietrich received the Swords (26) for his command of the Leibstandarte on the Russian Front.

On 6 June 1944, the Allied armies invaded France, and once again the Leibstandarte saw some furious combat, in which its units enhanced their fighting reputation even further, Dietrich winning the coveted Diamonds on 6 August 1944.

Already disillusioned by Hitler's conduct of the war, Dietrich was given

'Panzermeyer' — Kurt Meyer — extreme right, with Heinrich Springer, Gerd Bremer and 'Sepp' Dietrich at the Field Headquarters of the Leibstandarte, in Russia, June 1942.

command of 6 SS-Panzer Army during the ill fated Ardennes Offensive, after which the Leibstandarte was ordered to Hungary in a vain attempt to halt the Soviet advance. During the closing stages of the war, the Leibstandarte moved into Austria where it surrendered to US Forces.

Dietrich's military career closely paralleled the successes of his beloved Leibstandarte, and it was as a result of the shooting of US prisoners of war by troops under his command (though not on his direct orders) at Malmedy during the Ardennes Offensive that he was charged with war crimes at Dachau in 1946. However, his life sentence was commuted after allegations of misconduct of the trial. He was released in 1955.

In 1957 he was imprisoned again, this time by West German authorities for his part in the so-called 'Night of the Long Knives' when Ernst Röhm and other senior SA leaders were liquidated on Hitler's orders. Released eighteen months later, Dietrich went into retirement, but kept in close touch with veterans of the Leibstandarte until his death in 1966. His funeral was attended by many thousands of his former comrades.

17. **Generalfeldmarschall Walter Model** Born in 1891, Model served with an Infantry unit during World War One and by the end of the war was a Hauptmann on the General Staff. Retained in the Reichswehr after the war, Model had risen to the rank of Generalmajor by the eve of World War Two.

Model served as a staff officer during the Polish and French Campaigns before being given command of 3 Panzer Division with the rank of Generalleutnant. The success of this unit brought Model promotion to full General and, with this rank, command of XXXI Panzer Corps. On numerous occasions Model openly argued with Hitler over how various actions should be fought. Far from causing him trouble, his steadfast adherence to his principles earned him Hitler's respect and he rapidly became one of Hitler's most dependable Generals, with the nickname 'The Führer's Fireman', being constantly rushed back and forward to various sectors of the front where his leadership more often than not saved the day.

Model's superb command of strategy and tactics earned him the Knight's Cross on 9 July 1941, the Oakleaves (74) on 17 February 1942, and the Swords (28) on 2 April 1943. The debacle at Stalingrad, however, brought about a temporary fall from favour for Model when he protested that the exhausted German Armies were in no fit state for any further offensive actions against the Soviets. Model, now a Generaloberst, was recalled to Germany in disgrace. However, the deteriorating situation on the Eastern Front meant that Hitler could not do without Model's experience and expertise for long, and he was soon recalled to the front to take over command of Army Group North, whose position was becoming desperate. The success which Model enjoyed in saving this situation once again earned him promotion to Feldmarschall by a grateful Hitler. Over the next few months Model was to prove his worth time and time again, at one time commanding over one hundred Divisions at once.

On 17 August 1944, whilst commanding Army Group 'Centre' on the Russian Front, Model was awarded the Diamonds, and transferred to the Western Front where even his skills could only delay but not stop the inevitable advance of the Allied invasion forces. He was, however, responsible for the troops which inflicted the defeat at Arnhem on the advancing British and American Airborne Armies.

Model also played a part in the Ardennes Offensive, which he himself had always felt doomed to failure. The subsequent weakening of the German Armies on the Western Front could only hasten the now inevitable defeat of Germany but Model persisted in his steadfast defence

Generalfeldmarschall Walter Model, in leather greatcoat, consults with General der Fallschirmjäger Eugen Meindl on the Western Front, 1944. Meindl wears the 'Kreta' cuffband.

until the end. On 21 April 1945, Generalfeldmarschall Model, one of Germany's finest soldiers committed suicide. Model feared that he might be handed over to the Soviets on Germany's surrender, a fate which many Germans regarded as worse than death.

The military tradition of the Model family continues however, and Model's son, Hans-Georg, is serving at the time of writing as a Brigade-General commanding 7 Panzergrenadierbrigade of the West German Army.

18. **Major Erich Hartmann** The highest scoring fighter pilot in history, Erich 'Bubi' Hartmann ran up an incredible score of three hundred and fifty-two victories within a period of just over two years. Like Rudel, Hartmann preferred to get as close to his target as possible before opening fire, to increase the chances of success, despite the increased danger. He was awarded the Knight's Cross on 4 July 1944, the Oakleaves (420) on 2 March 1944, and the Swords (75) on 4 July 1944. Hartmann's Diamonds

were awarded on 25 August 1944 after his total score had reached three hundred and one.

At the war's end Hartmann was handed over by the US forces who captured him to the Soviets and spent ten years in captivity. On his release he found that his skills were still in demand by his fatherland, and he was re-commissioned into the West German Luftwaffe in which he served until retiring with the rank of Oberstleutnant.

19. **General Der Panzertruppe Hermann Balck.** Hermann Balck was awarded the Knight's Cross on 3 June 1940, the Oakleaves (155) on 22 December 1942, the Swords (25) on 4 March 1943, and the Diamonds on 31 August 1944. He was a much respected and able officer whose devotion to duty and the well being of his men far exceeded any concern for his own safety. Balck's Diamonds came whilst he was commander of 4 Panzerarmee on the Eastern Front.

20. **General Der Fallschirmtruppe Bernhard-Hermann Ramcke** A popular leader of Germany's elite 'Fallschirmjäger', 'Papa' Ramcke having been awarded the Knight's Cross on 21 August 1941, and the Oakleaves (145) on 15 November 1942, was given the distinction of receiving the Swords (99) and Diamonds simultaneously, on 20 September 1944, in recognition of his defence of the Brest Fortress area in France, as fortress commander. Ramcke survived the war and died in retirement at the age of seventy-nine.

21. **Major Heinz-Wolfgang Schnaufer** Schnaufer was awarded the Knight's Cross on 15 January 1944, the Oakleaves (507) on 27 June 1944, and the Swords (84) on 30 July 1944, and was decorated with the Diamonds on 16 October 1944 after scoring his one hundredth victory flying with NJG1. Schnaufer was one of the Luftwaffe's most successful night fighter pilots. He is credited with shooting down nine bombers in a single night, and on one occasion shot down five heavy bombers in fourteen minutes. Feared and respected by the aircrews of RAF Bomber Command, he was known as 'The Ghost of St Trond'. Schnaufer ended the war in command of Nachtjagdgeschwader 4, with one hundred and twenty-one victories. He was killed in a road accident in 1950.

22. **Fregattenkapitän Albrecht Brandi** Brandi was decorated with the Knight's Cross on 21 January 1943, and received the Oakleaves (224) less than four months later, on 11 April 1943. He was awarded the Swords (66) on 13 May 1944. As commander of *U-967,* Brandi received the Diamonds on 24 November 1944 after having sunk a total of 115,000 tons of Allied

shipping, including the incredible tally of twelve destroyers! After the award of the Diamonds, Brandi was promoted from Korvettenkapitän to Fregattenkapitän, and given command of the Kleinkampfverbande in Holland. He died in Cologne in 1966 at the age of fifty-one.

23. **Generalfeldmarschall Ferdinand Schörner** Awarded the Knight's Cross on 20 April 1941, Schörner was decorated with the Oakleaves (398) on 17 February 1944, and the Swords (93) on 28 August 1944. A staunch believer in the Nazi cause, Schörner's political beliefs did not prevent him from standing up to Hitler and arguing against his decisions when he felt justified in doing so. As commander Army Group North, he was decorated with the Diamonds on 1 January 1945 in recognition of his command of the units involved in the defensive actions in Kurland. He was promoted to Generalfeldmarschall on 5 April 1945.

24. **General Der Panzertruppe Hasso Eccard von Manteuffel** Born in Potsdam in 1897, von Manteuffel joined the cavalry after leaving cadet

Hitler congratulates Hasso von Manteuffel at the Führer Headquarters, 1944. Manteuffel wears the Panzer Battle Badge on the breast pocket, the 'Afrika' campaign cufftitle on his right cuff and the 'Grossdeutschland' sleeveband.

school and served in this branch of the armed services during world War One. After the war, he remained a staunch cavalryman, but was a firm believer in the advantages of armoured warfare.

During the opening of the invasion of Soviet Russia, he commanded Schutzen Regiment 6 of 7 Panzer Division and was awarded the Knight's Cross on 31 December 1941 in recognition of his unit's capture of a bridge over the Volga-Moscow canal in November of that year.

By November of the following year, von Manteuffel commanded 7 Panzer Division and served in the North African theatre of operations against the British before being transferred once again to the Eastern Front, where in November 1943 his troops were responsible for the recapture of the heavily defended town of Shitomir from the Soviets. For this action he received the Oakleaves (332) on 23 November.

The following month, von Manteuffel was given command of the élite 'Grossdeutschland' Division and fought a long series of defensive actions against the Soviets, often against huge odds, repulsing numerous Soviet attacks. 'Grossdeutschland' retreated gradually into East Prussia and in early 1944 counter-attacked against the enemy in the Kiev salient. For his command of 'Grossdeutschland' during this period, he became the fiftieth recipient of the Swords, on 22 February 1944. Until the end of his military career, von Mateuffel wore the coveted 'Grossdeutschland' sleeveband in memory of his service with the army's premier division.

He was transferred to the Western Front and given command of 5 Panzerarmee. During the Ardennes Offensive, with which von Manteuffel disagreed, 5 Panzerarmee made excellent progress until halted by a combination of lack of fuel, ammunition, and equipment and poorly trained troops. General von Manteuffel had argued that the Ardennes Offensive plans were far too ambitious and that they should be modified. Nevertheless, his successes during the early part of the so-called 'Battle of the Bulge' gained him the Diamonds on 18 February 1945.

After the war, von Manteuffel, having earned the honour and respect of his enemies as well as his friends, and with his name and reputation untarnished, served three years in the West German Bundestag before his retirement. He died of a heart attack in 1978.

25. **Generalmajor Theodor Tolsdorff** Tolsdorff was awarded the Knight's Cross on 20 November 1941, the Oakleaves (302) on 15 May 1943, and the Swords (80) on 18 July 1944. Generalmajor Tolsdorff, commanding 340 Volksgrenadier Division, received the Diamonds on 18 March 1945 in recognition of his division's achievements during the Ardennes Offensive. His personal bravery is well attested to by the fact that he was wounded in action no less than fourteen times.

26. **Generalleutnant Dr Karl Maus** Maus received the Knight's Cross on 26 November 1941, and was awarded the Oakleaves (335) on 24 November 1943, and then the Swords (101) on 23 November 1944. He commanded the 7 Panzer Division on the Russian Front and was decorated with the Diamonds on 15 April 1945 for his bravery in action. His Diamonds were awarded whilst he was still in hospital recovering from wounds sustained during heavy fighting at the front. He survived the war and died in 1959 at the age of sixty.

27. **General Der Panzertruppe Dietrich von Saucken** The Knight's Cross was awarded to von Saucken on 15 January 1942, the Oakleaves (281) on 22 February 1943, and the Swords (46) on 20 February 1944. The final recipient of the Diamonds, von Sauken (Armee Oberkommando 'Ostpreussen') had his award authorised on 9 May 1945 by Grossadmiral Dönitz. This was the only award of the Diamonds made by the short-lived Dönitz regime.

THE GOLDEN OAKLEAVES, SWORDS AND DIAMONDS

This decoration was instituted by Hitler on 29 December 1944 to reward the exceptional achievements of Stuka ace Oberst Hans-Ulrich Rudel. By this time Oberst Rudel had won every decoration for gallantry which Germany had, yet he had continued to achieve outstanding success with his Stuka Geschwader 'Immelmann' on the Russian Front.

At a time when the Luftwaffe had fallen from grace in the eyes of Hitler, the creation of a new award prompted by the heroism of a Luftwaffe officer was a source of great pleasure to Göring. Hitler had intended to limit the award of this new decoration to a maximum of twelve, but, in fact, only Oberst Rudel had received this decoration by the time the war ended.

The decoration consisted of a set of hand crafted eighteen carat gold Swords and Oakleaves produced by the Godet firm in Berlin. The clasp was set with fifty small diamonds on the oakleaves and the sword hilts. As far as is known, no special award document was produced, due to the late date of the award, 1 January 1945.

Hans-Ulrich Rudel Born in 1916 in Silesia, Hans-Ulrich Rudel joined the fledgling Luftwaffe at the age of twenty. He received his first posting to a Stuka Geschwades in 1938, as an officer cadet. In contrast to his later experiences, Rudel's early years in the Luftwaffe were relatively quiet. He was, by his own admission, no star pupil. His superiors were wary of allowing him into action during the early campaigns, and he was forced to

Opposite
Rudel's beautiful Golden Oakleaves Swords and Diamonds.

Oberst Rudel's decorations are well displayed in this photograph and include the German Cross in Gold, Pilot's Badge, Pilot Observer's Badge with Diamonds, Iron Cross First Class, Flight Clasp in Platinum with Diamonds and, of course, the Knight's Cross with Golden Swords Oakleaves and Diamonds.

control his impatience and desire for action until after the invasion of the Soviet Union in 1941.

Once he had shown his superiors that his ability as a pilot was not in question he was quickly accepted by his comrades, though his habit of diving to extremely low levels to ensure hits on his targets greatly worried his superiors.

His tactics paid off, however. When his Squadron attacked the Soviet battleship *Marat* in September 1941, it was Rudel's Stuka which did the real damage, seriously crippling the warship. A few days later, Rudel finished the job when a 2000lb bomb from his Stuka made a direct hit on *Marat,* breaking her back. This success was just the beginning of an incredible succession of achievements by this legendary pilot.

The first man in his squadron to win the Deutsche Kreuz in Gold, Rudel added the Knight's Cross to his honours in January 1942 after flying more than four hundred missions, and achieving great success against Soviet warships and in bombing missions against Soviet held bridges.

Rudel soon ran up a huge number of combat flights and in accordance with Luftwaffe policy, was removed from front line service and assigned to a training unit to give the benefit of his experience to new pilots. Rudel hated being removed from the front line and, after spending some time in this training unit, persuaded his superiors to transfer him back to combat duty.

Rudel's total of combat flights continued to grow and he was once again removed from the front, this time being sent to an experimental unit, flying the new 'tank busting' version of the Ju 87 Stuka which was equipped with two 3.7cm cannon. Rudel was honoured with the Oakleaves to his Knight's Cross in April 1943 after flying over one thousand missions, but refused to accept it unless he was permitted to transfer back to a combat unit. He won his argument.

By November of 1942, with his hundredth victory and over 1600 missions flown, Rudel's successes with his tank busting Stukas had brought him the award of the Swords. At the same time, Rudel's faithful rear gunner, Henschel, was due to be awarded the Knight's Cross, but red tape had delayed matters. In typical Rudel style, he got round the matter by simply taking Henschel with him to the award ceremony at Hitler's headquarters, whereupon Hitler promptly conferred the Knight's Cross on Henschel.

As his successes continued to mount, Rudel had a number of close calls, including being shot down behind enemy lines and only just managing to escape to safety.

In March 1944 he was awarded the coveted Diamonds, and once again refused to accept them unless he was permitted to stay with his unit. Once again this was agreed. As his achievements continued, and his score of victories mounted, he was honoured with the Pilot/Observer's Badge with Diamonds, and the Front Flight Clasp for an incredible 2000 combat missions, but refused to accept it unless he was permitted to transfer back to a combat unit. He won his argument.

Much to Reichsmarschall Göring's glee, it soon became clear that Rudel's achievements had reached a stage where a special award would have to be created for him — he had already won every other gallantry award the state could offer. Hitler created a special award, the Golden Oakleaves, Swords and Diamonds. Incredibly, Rudel once again refused to accept unless he was permitted to stay with his unit, and once again this was agreed. This agreement was soon overturned once Hitler had had second thoughts. It made no difference to Rudel however, who continued to fly anyway. His kills were credited to the squadron as a whole in an attempt to disguise the fact that he was still flying.

Rudel's luck could not hold out for ever. His injuries from another crash were so bad that a leg had to be amputated. Amazingly, even this did not stop him, and he was soon back with his beloved squadron where he served the last few remaining weeks of the war before surrendering to the Americans.

Rudel's final score included 2530 missions flown, five hundred and nineteen enemy tanks destroyed, one battleship, one cruiser and one destroyer sunk, and seventy other craft sunk or damaged. Twenty-six of his tank kills were made when flying with only one leg.

Oberst Rudel survived the war, and became a successful businessman.

THE KNIGHT'S CROSS AWARD DOCUMENTS

On the award of a Knight's Cross of the Iron Cross being approved, the recipient was notified by means of a preliminary certificate, a Vorlaufiges Besitzzeugnis. This was a simple printed document onto which was typed the particulars of the recipient. As can be seen from the examples illsutrated, these documents are similar in format to the award documents for the Iron Cross First and Second Classes.

This document, in the early days of the war at least, was followed by an elaborate citation, or Urkunde. This citation was beautifully hand lettered on parchment vellum and contained in a hand made binder or case.

Hitler considered these Ritterkreuzurkunden to be of great importance. He assembled a team of artisans to manufacture the award documents. Professor Gerdy Troost was in overall charge of the manufacturing process. Lettering was performed by Franziska Kobell and leatherwork by

Preliminary Notification Document for the Knight's Cross of the Iron Cross. Both Gothic and block letter patterns of this type are known.

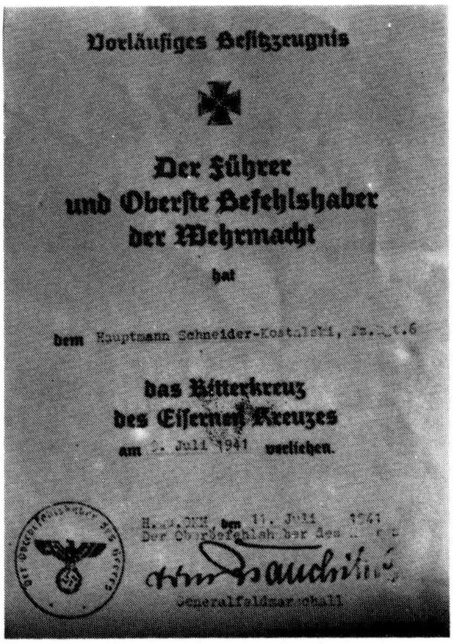
Vorläufiges Besitzzeugnis

Der Führer
und Oberste Befehlshaber
der Wehrmacht
hat

dem Hauptmann Schneider-Kostalski

das Ritterkreuz
des Eisernen Kreuzes
am 2. Juli 1941 verliehen.

H.Qu.OKH, den 11. Juli 1941

Generalfeldmarschall

Variant of the Knight's Cross Preliminary Notification Document with alternative text.

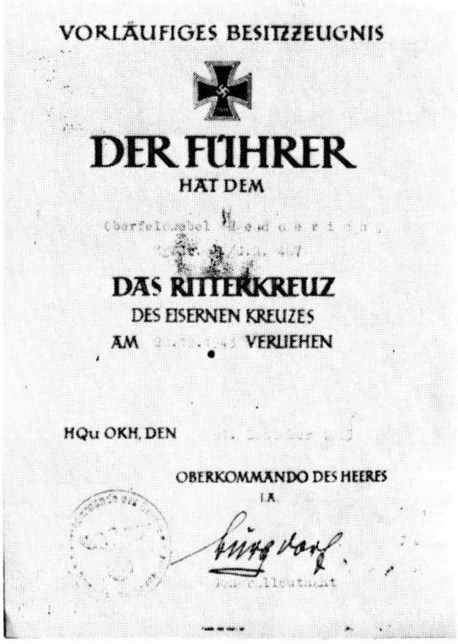
VORLÄUFIGES BESITZZEUGNIS

DER FÜHRER
HAT DEM

Oberfeldwebel

DAS RITTERKREUZ
DES EISERNEN KREUZES
AM VERLIEHEN

HQu OKH, DEN

OBERKOMMANDO DES HEERES
I.A.

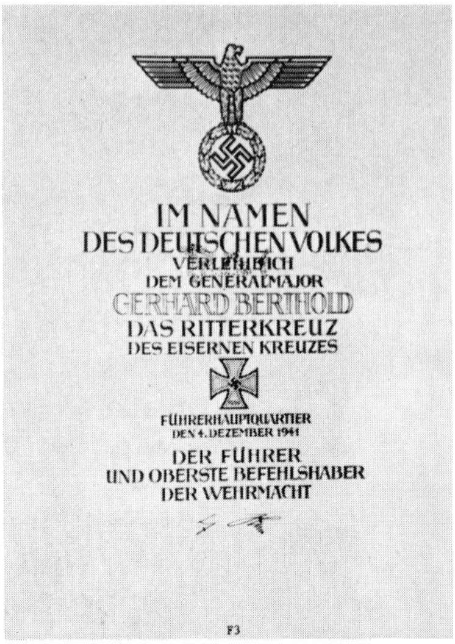

IM NAMEN
DES DEUTSCHEN VOLKES
VERLEIHE ICH
DEM GENERALMAJOR
GERHARD BERTHOLD
DAS RITTERKREUZ
DES EISERNEN KREUZES

FÜHRERHAUPTQUARTIER
DEN 4. DEZEMBER 1941

DER FÜHRER
UND OBERSTE BEFEHLSHABER
DER WEHRMACHT

F3

Urkunde for the Knight's Cross to an army Generalmajor.

Frieda Thiersch. Gold work was carried out by Franz and Hermann Wandinger. Each citation bore the signature of Adolf Hitler.

The Knight's Cross citation was lettered in red-brown ink with the name of the recipient in Gold leaf. It was contained in a binder which was covered in red leather bearing the national emblem embossed in gold leaf. The inside lining was in parchment, and the binder's name, Frieda Thiersch, is normally found on the lower inside rear cover.

The Oakleaves citation is similar to that for the Knight's Cross, but the national emblem is executed in gold leaf, like the recipient's name. The title of the award on the citation is altered to read DAS EICHENLAUB ZUM RITTERKREUZ. This and subsequent citations also omit the small Iron Cross motif. The binder for the oakleaves is covered in white parchment and bears a gilt metal national emblem in the centre.

The Oakleaves and Swords citation also has the name and national emblem in gold leaf, with the rest of the text in red-brown ink. The title of the award is amended to read DAS EICHENLAUB MIT SCHWERTERN ZUM RITTERKREUZ. The document is contained in a case rather than a binder. The case is covered in white parchment, and the lid features a gilt metal national emblem and gilt metal geometric pattern edging.

The citation for the Diamonds is very elaborate indeed. The entire text is executed in gold and framed with gilt tooled leather. The case is covered with morocco leather of a colour to suit the branch of the armed forces in which the recipient served, red, navy blue, and grey-blue for the army, navy and Luftwaffe, respectively. In the centre is a gilt metal national

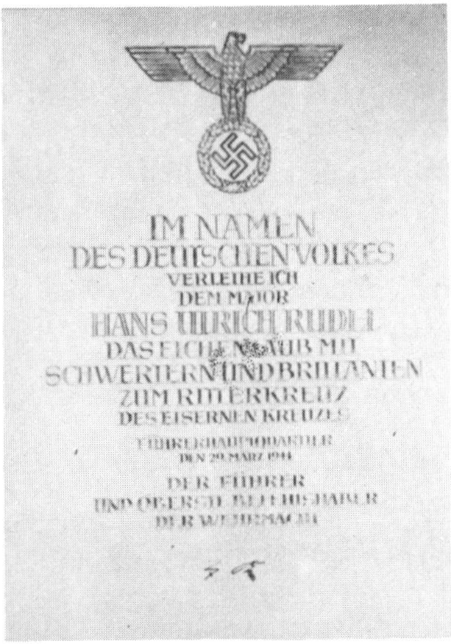
IM NAMEN
DES DEUTSCHEN VOLKES
VERLEIHE ICH
DEM MAJOR
HANS ULRICH RUDEL
DAS EICHENLAUB MIT
SCHWERTERN UND BRILLANTEN
ZUM RITTERKREUZ
DES EISERNEN KREUZES
DER FÜHRER

Above
The cover for the case for Rudel's Diamonds Urkunde. Covered in blue morocco leather with gilt metal ornamentation, it features diamond chips on the swastika.

Above left
Urkunde for the Diamonds to Oberst Rudel. The entire text is lettered in gold.

Left
The cover for the case of Göring's Grand Cross Urkunde.

emblem with the swastika bearing a number of small diamonds. The edge features a gilt metal geometric pattern design.

The Grand Cross citation was likewise entirely executed in gold on parchment with a gilt tooled leather frame. The case was similar to that for the Diamonds but had a much more elaborate edging set with numerous precious stones.

Mention should also be made of a special binder for Knight's Cross citations to officers of Feldmarschall rank. It was identical to that for the basic Knight's Cross citation but for the addition of a very elaborate geometric edging featuring interwoven swastikas and Iron Crosses.

In February 1984, Christie's auction house of London sold the Urkunde for Hans-Ulrich Rudel's basic Knight's Cross — not for the famous Golden Oakleaves, or even one of the other additions — for an astonishing £22,000! Normally, citations are sold for about one tenth of this sum, but, while it still seems inflated, the price was obviously paid because of who Rudel was.

The Grand Cross of the Iron Cross of 1939

Instituted on 1 September 1939, the Grand Cross was designed along the same lines as its predecessors. The obverse and reverse designs are the same as for the Second Class, but the Grand Cross is, of course, much

Opposite
Hermann Göring, the sole recipient of the 1939 Grand Cross, seen here at the time of his capture. The *Pour le Mérite* is worn much lower than the Grand Cross.

An original Grand Cross of the Iron Cross, removed from Göring's property at the end of the war.

Pre-war photographs of Göring often show him proudly sporting his *Pour le Mérite*..

An embroidered wire version of the 1939 Star to the Grand Cross. No information is available on this unusual piece, but it appears to be an original contemporary item.

Star to the Grand Cross of the Iron Cross 1939. The Iron Cross is affixed to the Sta by four rivets.

larger, at 63mm. Originally it was intended to have the outer edges of the frame in gold, but this was altered before the piece was ever awarded. A 57mm wide neck ribbon was produced for the award. The Grand Cross was presented in a red leather covered case, embossed with the eagle and swastika in gold.

Only one example was awarded, to Reichsmarschall Hermann Göring to reward his command of the Luftwaffe during the campaigns in France and the Low Countries in 1940. It is clear from photographs of Göring that he wore his Grand Cross from a much narrower ribbon than the 57mm width intended, and that he had a non-regulation solid suspension loop produced for his award.

Following the destruction of the Reichsmarschall's home and the loss of the original Grand Cross during an air raid on Berlin, Göring is said to have had an elaborate replica made. It was made with an onyx centre and platinum frame. It is known that Göring also had some duplicates of the original Cross. One of these is illustrated, courtesy of Forman Piccadilly Ltd. This piece has the makers mark of the Berlin firm of Godet as well as the silver content mark.

THE STAR TO THE GRAND CROSS

Whilst no Star to the 1939 Grand Cross was ever awarded, prototypes were certainly produced. They were manufactured by the Munich jewellers Rath, and consist of an eight pointed radiant star of solid silver. This is gilded but the gilding is so pale as to appear silver at first glance. Superimposed in the centre is a standard Iron Cross First Class, affixed by four small rivets.

The only known original example of this decoration was discovered by US Army intelligence officers in Austria at the end of the war. It was contained in a red leather case, the lid of which is set with an Iron Cross. The Star to the 1939 Grand Cross is now housed in the museum of the US Military Academy at West Point.

APPENDIX ONE: THE IRON CROSS OF 1957

After the defeat of Germany in 1945, all Third Reich decorations were prohibited. This situation lasted for twelve years, until 1957, when a new law was passed relating to the decorations of the Nazi Regime. The law permitted certain of these decorations to be worn again providing the swastika was removed. Initially, original badges were merely defaced by having the swastika broken or filed off. Eventually however, some of the firms which produced the original decorations began to manufacture the new versions with the designs altered to comply with the new laws.

The re-designed Iron Cross differs from the original 1939 version in that the swastika is replaced by a spray of oakleaves, similar to the reverse design of the original 1813 Iron Cross. Otherwise the design is unaltered. The Second Class, First Class and Knight's Crosses have been altered in

The post-1957 version of the 1939 Iron Cross featuring the Oakleaf Spray in place of the swastika.

Post-war version of the 1939 Knight's Cross with Swords and Oakleaves. The Swords and Oakleaves Clasp, where the sword hilts touch the opposing blade, is based on the wartime jeweller's copy.

Cased 1957 version of the 1939 Knight's Cross of the Iron Cross. The case is lined with white rather than black velvet.

Above right
General Matzky of the West German Army wears the 1957 version of his 1939 Knight's Cross.

Right
The current method of wear for 1939 Iron Crosses is more commonly in the form of ribbon bars as illustrated here. Top left is the Iron Cross Second Class with the First Class to the right. Below is the Ribbon of the Knight's Cross.

this way, but the Grand Cross has not, as the sole recipient, Hermann Göring, is dead.

The First and Second Class Bars have been totally redesigned and now bear a close resemblance to the 1914 Bar to the 1870 Iron Cross. The First Class Bar comprises a small rectangular bar bearing the date 1939 with a small Iron Cross motif in the centre. It has a horizontal brooch pin on the reverse. The Second Class is identical but has two prongs on the reverse. The Oakleaves, Swords and Oakleaves, etc, have not been changed, as they did not bear any Nazi motif. Those produced today are the same type as wartime jeweller's copies, ie the reverse of the Swords is plain, etc.

The new Knight's Crosses are made with either '800' silver or silver plate frames. They are generally devoid of the matt silver oxide effect to the beaded edge, as found on original 1939 Crosses. Although the new post war type of Iron Cross may be seen worn by surviving veterans on formal occasions, those who served in the West German army after the war more commonly wore their awards in the form of ribbon bars. The Iron Cross Second Class is worn as a ribbon only, the First Class is worn as a ribbon with a miniature Iron Cross device, and the Knight's Cross is worn as a wider ribbon with miniature Cross device.

The Deutsche Kreuz

One other award which now features the Iron Cross in its redesigned form is the Deutsche Kreuz (German Cross) in Gold, which was introduced in 1941 to bridge the gap between the Iron Cross First Class and the Knight's Cross, and some 17,000 were awarded. It is a large sunburst badge with an enamelled swastika centre surrounded by a wreath of oakleaves. It is a well-made, complex badge, constructed in four parts and was worn pinned to the right breast. Embroidered cloth versions were also popular.

The oakleaves surrounding the swastika are gold for combatant awards and silver for non-combatant. The silver version was usually awarded to recipients of the War Merit Cross First Class before the award of the Knight's Cross of the War Merit Cross. Not every Knight's Cross winner was awarded the German Cross in Gold. The currently produced version of the German Cross has the swastika replaced by a small Iron Cross. Aptly, the current version of the German Cross in Silver bears a miniature of the War Merit Cross First Class.

The post-war design for the Bar to the Iron Cross of both classes.

A selection of pins for wear on the lapel of civilian clothes. Included in the top row are, left to right, Knight's Cross, Honour Roll Clasp, Iron Cross First Class and Iron Cross Second Class.

APPENDIX TWO: THE LDO

During the Third Reich period, manufacturers of awards and decorations proliferated. As well as producing awards on a private basis, for example manufacturing commemorative pieces for individual units, many produced official state decorations. The design and manufacture of these awards was strictly controlled, and the manufacturers formed their own organisation, the Leistungsgemeinschaft deutscher Ordenshersteller (Association of German Orders Manufacturers), usually abbreviated to LDO.

Member firms of the LDO were allocated a manufacturer's code number or Herstellungszeichen. Unfortunately, the numbers were frequently changed round, so that the number alone cannot always identify the specific manufacture of an award. Additionally, some manufacturers never marked their produce at all. Many of the better quality awards, however, are found with these makers codes. These are usually prefixed with the letter L but occasionally only with the number.

Any recipient of an award could, at his own expense, purchase copies

The LDO monogram on the lid of a privately purchased cased Bar to the Iron Cross First Class.

The case for a privately purchased set of Oakleaves. The official issue box lid is devoid of markings.

through LDO outlets by providing proof that he was entitled to the award. A copy would normally come in a case or packet bearing the LDO logo, and with a small guarantee card offering free replacements should any item fail to satisfy.

The firms generally recognised as having produced some of the best quality awards include Godet of Berlin, Deschler of Munich, Steinhauer und Luck of Ludenscheid, and C E Juncker of Berlin.

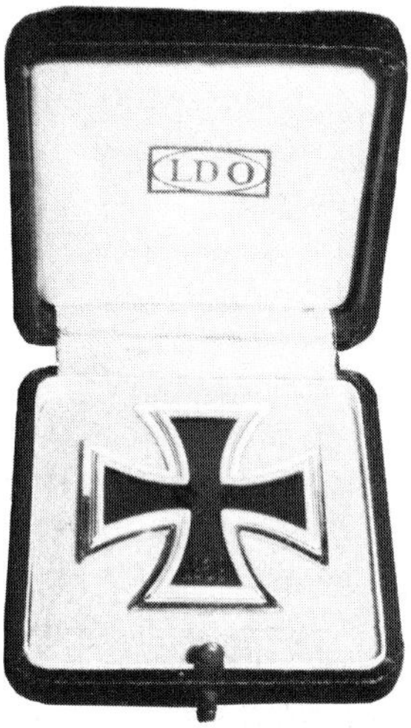

Privately purchased Oakleaves. The case interior is identical to the official award.

Above right
Privately purchased Iron Cross First Class showing the LDO logo inside the box lid.

A selection of the many different patterns of attachment devices found on privately acquired Crosses.

APPENDIX THREE: POST-WAR REPRODUCTIONS

The popularity of Iron Crosses, and especially Knights Crosses, with collectors has led to a huge increase in the value of genuine original pieces. Unfortunately, the rise in value has also led to an increase in the number of reproductions appearing for sale. A case can be made for the value of reproductions as 'space fillers' where original items are so rare or expensive that they are out of the reach of collectors, but the case can only be valid if reproductions are sold only as reproductions. Unfortunately, the better quality reproductions are all too often sold as genuine at a very high price to unsuspecting collectors. Of course, some are so accurate that it will

Reproduction Knight's Cross of the Iron Cross. Although visually acceptable, the piece is cast in one piece from a soft, easily bent alloy.

A totally false citation for the Knight's Cross with an equally fake cased award. Compare these with photographs of the real thing.

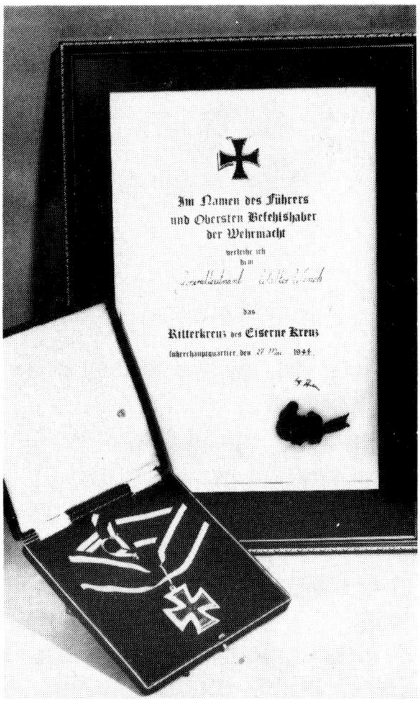

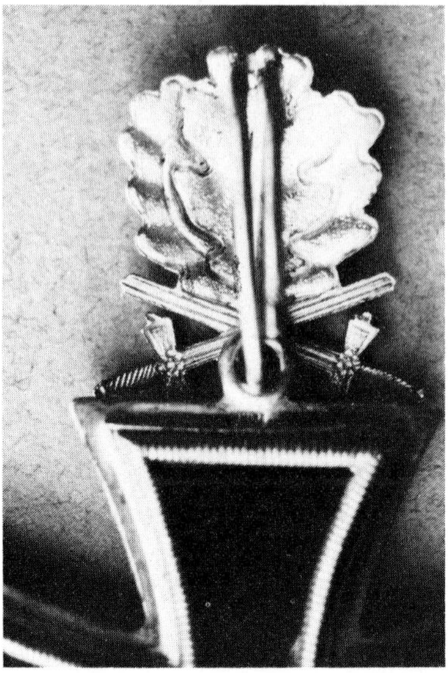

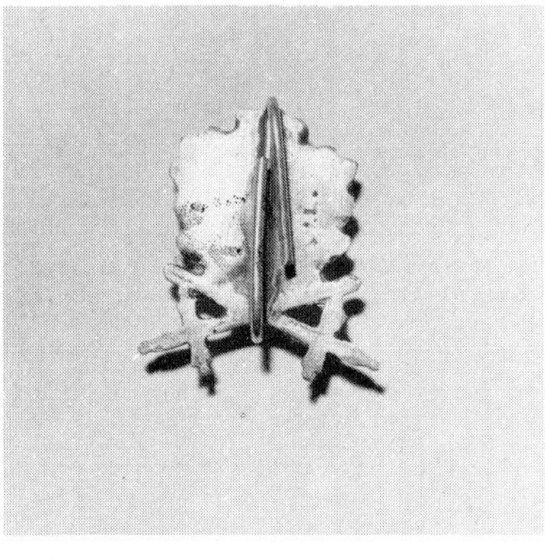

Close up of the reverse of the reproduction Swords and Oakleaves, stamped from thin sheet metal.

Above left
Reproduction Knight's Cross with Swords and Oakleaves by the Austrian firm of Souval. The space between the base of the Oakleaves and the Crossed Swords is solid.

Reverse of the fake cast Swords and Oaks. The crudity of the casting is quite obvious.

often be the case that the dealer himself may be unaware that he is selling a reproduction.

Basically, reproductions of the Knight's Cross fall into three broad categories.

1. Crude fakes. These are usually cast in one piece from soft alloys. Whilst some may appear accurate from a distance, few collectors would be taken in by them on close inspection. These are usually used in film or theatrical work.

2. Good Quality Reproductions. Prime example in this category is the firm of Rudolf Souval of Vienna. Souval was an authorised manufacturer

A fake cast set of Swords and Oakleaves in silver plated brass.

A fairly good quality Souval copy of the Knight's Cross with Swords Oakleaves and Diamonds. However, the silver content hallmark is incorrectly positioned on the *obverse* of the rim.

of awards during the period of the Third Reich, and still manufactures them today, often from the original tools. The modern pieces lack the quality of finish and are often in different metals to the originals. Souval's Knight's Crosses come with genuine silver or silver plated frames. They often carry the logo L/58 on the frame just below the eye for the ribbon loop. They lack the crispness of originals, particularly on the beaded edge. The swastika on original Knight's Crosses is normally of the same height as the beaded edge, but Souval's are much lower. However, all in all, they are of good quality and will fool many novice collectors.

3. High Quality Copies. These are the 'worst offenders'. Recently, some enterprising person has been altering post war Knight's Crosses by having them disassembled, the oakleaves removed, and a swastika added. As the 'raw material' is often a fine quality piece by, say Steinhauer und Luck, and as the results differ from the originals only in very minor points, these altered Knight's Cross forgeries are very difficult to detect, and, once aged, will pose many problems for accurate identification.

The Oakleaves and Swords and Oakleaves clasps are also being reproduced. These also come in a range of qualities from very crude brass castings which are then silver plated to good quality pieces which are fairly accurate but are stamped rather than die struck. These can be detected immediately as the originals have a smooth plain concave reverse. Also, these stamped pieces have the silver hallmark on the loop rather than on the reverse of the oakleaves as on the originals.

Unfortunately, there is no simple answer to the problem of reproductions. Only experience of handling and examining genuine pieces will give the collector confidence, but the rarity of many of the originals will make this very difficult. The best that collectors can do is to deal only with reputable businesses which have had experience in handling original items.

APPENDIX FOUR: COLLECTING AND RESTORING

After establishing that a particular Iron Cross is a genuine article, the enthusiast may wish to give further consideration to its value, condition, and suitability for inclusion in a collection. For those who wish to specialise in the Iron Cross in general, most genuine examples encountered may be considered as suitable additions to a collection, but it is obviously unlikely that a specialist in World War Two decorations would wish to add Franco-Prussian War medals to a collection. Alternatively, one may specialise in collecting examples of the decorations known to have been won by a particular personality.

Having decided to aquire a specific example, the collector will wish to consider its price and condition. It is pointless spending hard-earned cash on the purchase of a common 1939 Iron Cross if it is in poor condition, because examples in excellent to near mint condition are not difficult to find. On the other hand, original examples of the 1813 Iron Cross are so rare that most collectors would jump at the chance of even a damaged or badly worn specimen. Prices change so rapidly with inflation that it would be pointless to suggest prices for the range of Iron Crosses: they would be out of date before this book has even been published. However, a table of comparative rarities is appended to this section, but it should be noted that these are approximate, as it is quite possible for a rare variant of a common type of Iron Cross to be worth more than the standard version of a scarce award.

Having decided that a particular piece warrants purchase even if a little 'run down', most collectors will at least *consider* whether to try to 'restore' it to some of its former glory. This is a matter of personal preference. Some purists would recoil in horror at the thought of cleaning up a medal or decoration, but no soldier would wear badly tarnished decorations 'on parade'. Once again, however, it is wise to err on the side of caution and avoid working on a piece which is particularly valuable or fragile.

I have personally used the following restoration method successfully on a number of 1939 pieces and some 1914 pieces.

Stage One. Clean the piece thoroughly with warm soapy water and an old, soft toothbrush. In some cases this will be all that is required to remove surface dirt.

Stage Two. Immerse the award in a proprietary brand of silver cleaner such as Goddards 'Silver Dip' (do not use any abrasive cleaners). This will remove tarnish and, in the cases of many 1939 pieces, will clean up the matt oxide finish beautifully. Rinse in water afterwards.

Stage Three. Dry thoroughly, preferably using a hair dryer, which will prevent water being trapped under the beaded edge and rusting the centre. The edges can then be lightly buffed with a soft cloth.

If the black finish to the centre is damaged, this is best left alone, particularly with a painted finish. Do not attempt to repaint with a paintbrush because this will merely leave brushmarks to spoil the finish. A good quality airbrush as used by modellers can do a good job, but plenty of practise on a 'scrapper' will be required before risking a good piece. Some Iron Crosses with chemically blackened centres may be restored successfully using commercially available gun blacking from your local gunsmith.

These tips may be helpful, but should not be taken as *suggestions*. Only the collector with the award in his hands can make the decision as to

A nicely displayed collection of Iron Crosses ranging from 1813 to 1957. Top left, 1813; bottom left, 1870: centre, 1939; top right, 1957: bottom right, 1914.

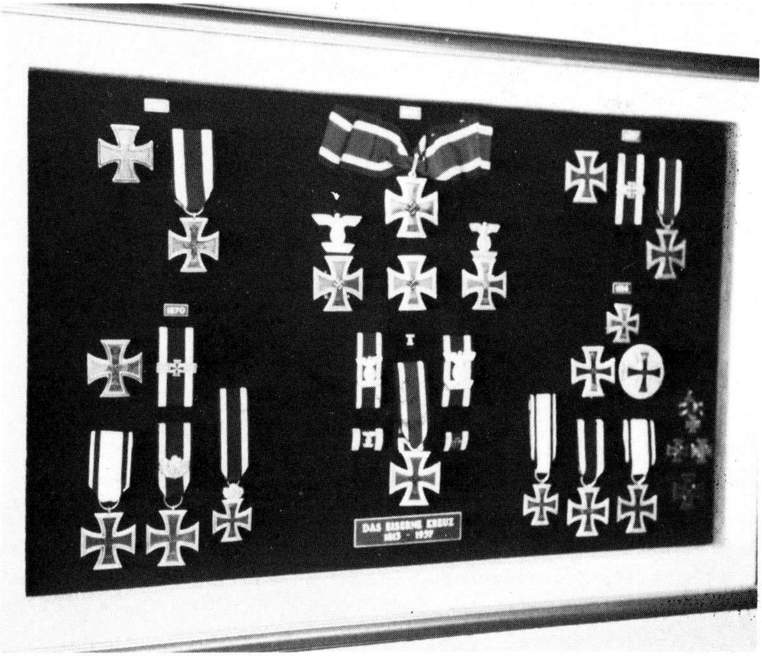

whether to attempt to restore it. If a positive decision is made, please practise first on a damaged or otherwise valueless piece before risking a 'good one'. In the final analysis, the best advice is probably — 'If in doubt, don't'.

Exceedingly Rare	*Very Rare*	*Rare*	*Very Scarce*	*Scarce*	*Common*
1813 Grand Cross*					
1813 First Class	1813 Second Class				
Blücherstern*					
Kulm Cross*					
1870 Grand Cross*	1870 First Class	1870 Second Class			
		'25' Oakleaves			
1914 Grand Cross					1914 Second Class
1914 Star*					1914 First Class
1914 Bar to 1870 Cross					
Hildegard Orden*					
1939 Grand Cross					
Golden Oakleaves/Swords/Diamonds					
Oakleaves/Swords/Diamonds	Oakleaves/Swords	Knight's Cross	1939 Small Pattern	1939 First and Second Class Bars	1939 First Class
1939 Star*	Oakleaves	Cloth 1939 First Class	2nd Class Bar	1939 Second Class Bar	1939 Second Class

* These items are so rare as to be virtually unobtainable, and the only pieces likely to be encountered are museum copies.

COMPARATIVE RANKS

British	German		
Army	**Army/Air Force**	**Navy**	**Waffen-SS**
Private	Grenadier/Flieger	Matrose	SS-Schutze
-	Obergrenadier	-	SS-Oberschutze
Lance-Corporal	Gefreiter	Matrosengefreiter	SS-Sturmmann
-	Obergefreiter	Matrosenobergefr.	SS-Rottenführer
-	Stabsgefreiter	Matrosenhauptgefr.	-
-	-	Matrosenstabsgefr.	-
Corporal	Unteroffizier	Maat	SS-Unterscharführer
Sergeant	Unterfeldwebel	Obermaat	SS-Scharführer
Staff Sgt.	Feldwebel	Feldwebel	SS-Oberscharführer
W O Class 2	Oberfeldwebel	Stabsfeldwebel	SS-Hauptscharführer
-	Hauptfeldwebel	Oberfeldwebel	SS-Stabsscharführer
W O Class 1	Stabsfeldwebel	Stabsoberfeldwebel	SS-Sturmscharführer
Second Lieutenant	Leutnant	Leutnant zur See	SS-Untersturmführer
First Lieutenant	Oberleutnant	Oberleutnant zur See	SS-Obersturmführer
Captain	Hauptmann	Kapitänleutnant	SS-Hauptsturmführer
Major	Major	Korvettenkapitän	SS-Sturmbannführer
Lieutenant-Colonel	Oberstleutnant	Fregattenkapitän	SS-Obersturmbannführer
Colonel	Oberst	Kapitän zur See	SS-Standartenführer
-	-	Kommodore	SS-Oberführer
Brigadier	-	-	SS-Brigadeführer
Major General	Generalmajor	Vizeadmiral	SS-Gruppenführer
Lieutenant General	Generalleutnant	Konteradmiral	SS-Obergruppenführer
General	General	Admiral	SS-Oberstgruppenführer
-	Generaloberst	Generaladmiral	-
Field Marshall	Generalfeldmarschall	Grossadmiral	Reichsführer-SS

GLOSSARY

Abzeichen	Insignia, Badge
Armeegruppe	Army Group
Artillerie	Artillery
Aufklärung	Reconnaisance
Auszeichnung	Award, Decoration
Abteilung	Detachment, Squad
Band	Ribbon
Bataillon	Battalion
Besitzzeugnis	Certificate of Possession
Bundeswehr	Federal German Armed Forces
Bundesmarine	Federal German Navy
Eichenlaub	Oakleaves
Eisernes Kreuz	Iron Cross
Etui	Case
Fallschirmjäger	Paratroops
Feldbluse	Field Blouse
Feldmutze	Field Cap
Festung	Fortress
Flott	Fleet
Flotille	Flotilla
Gebirgsjäger	Mountain Troops
Generalstab	General Staff
Geschwader	Air Force Wing
Grosskreuz	Grand Cross
Gruppe	Group
Hakenkreuz	Swastika
Halsband	Neck Ribbon
Heer	Army

Hoheitszeichen	National Emblem, 1933-45 (the eagle and swastika)
HJ: Hitlerjugend	The Hitler Youth
Infanterie	Infantry
Jagdflieger	Fighter Pilot
Jäger	Rifleman
JG: Jagdgeschwader	Fighter Wing
Kaiser	Emperor
Kaiserliche	Imperial
Kavallerie	Cavalry
Kampfgruppe	Battle Group
KG: Kampfgeschwader	Bomber Squadron
Kommandeur	Commander
Kommodore	Air Force Wing Commander
Kriegsmarine	Navy (Third Reich Period)
LAH or LSSAH	Standard abbreviation for the Leibstandarte-SS 'Adolf Hitler'
Luftwaffe	German Air Force
NJG: Nachtjagdgeschwader	Night Fighter Wing
Oberbefehlshaber	Commander-in-Chief
OKL	Oberkommando der Luftwaffe (Airforce High Command)
OKH	Oberkommando des Heeres (Army High Command)
OKM	Oberkommando der Marine (Naval High Command)
OKW	Oberkommando der Wehrmacht (Armed Forces High Command)
Offizier	Officer
Ordensschnalle	Medal Ribbon Mounting
Panzergrenadier	Armoured Infantry
Pionier	Sapper
Ritterkreuz	Knight's Cross

Schwertern	Swords
Spange	Clasp, Bar
SS-Verfügungstruppe	SS Special Purpose Troops, the original Waffen-SS combat units
Staffel	Squadron
StuG:	Stutzkampfgeschwader
Stuka	(Dive Bomber) Squadron
Träger	Bearer (eg Ritterkreuzträger, Eichenlaubträger)
Urkunde	Citation
Verleihungstüte	Award Packet
Waffen-SS	SS Combat Troops
Wehrmacht	Armed Forces
Zerstörer	Destroyer (heavy fighter, eg Bf 110)
ZG: Zerstörergeschwader	Destroyer Squadron
Zug	Platoon

SELECT METRIC/ IMPERIAL EQUIVALENTS

mm	inches	mm	inches
1	0.0394	42	1.65
4	0.16	43	1.69
7.5	0.30	44	1.73
10	0.39	45	1.77
12.5	0.49	48	1.89
18	0.71	55	2.16
25	0.98	57	2.24
26	1.02	63	2.49
27	1.06	64	2.52
28	1.10	77	3.03
30	1.18	82	3.23
32	1.26	85	3.35
33	1.30	107	4.21
39	1.54	155	6.10
41	1.61	160	6.31

BIBLIOGRAPHY

Angolia, John R, *For Fuhrer and Fatherland*, Vol. 1, Bender Publishing, San Jose, USA (1976).

Angolia, John R, *On the Field of Honour*, Vol. 1, Bender Publishing, San Jose, USA (1979).

Angolia, John R, *On the Field of Honour,* Vol. 2, Bender Publishing, San Jose, USA (1980)

Davis, Brian L, *Badges and Insignia of the Third Reich 1933–1945*, Blandford Press, Poole, Dorset, UK (1983).

Feuerstein, Erwin, *Mit und Ohne Ritterkreuz*, Motorbuch Verlag, Stuttgart, (1974).

Hieronymussen, Paul, *Orders, Medals and Decorations of Britain and Europe in Colour,* Blandford Press, Poole, Dorset, UK (1967).

Kleitmann, Dr Kurt G, *Deutsche Auszeichnungen*, Die Ordens Sammlung, Berlin (1971).

Littlejohn, David & Dodkins, Col. C M, *Orders Decorations Medals and Badges of the Third Reich*, Bender Publishing, San Jose, USA (1968).

Möller-Witten, Hanns, *Mit dem Eichenlaub zum Ritterkreuz*, Erich Pabel Verlag, Rastatt, 1962.

Obermaier, Ernst, *Die Ritterkreuzträger der Luftwaffe*, Dieter Hoffmann Verlag, Mainz (1966).

Obermaier, Ernst, *Die Ritterkreuzträger der Luftwaffe*, Vol. 2. Dieter Hoffmann Verlag, Mainz, (1975).

Prowse, Anthony E, *The Iron Cross of Prussia and Germany*, privately published, (1971).

Range, Clemens, *Die Ritterkreuzträger der Kriegsmarine*, Motorbuch Verlag, Stuttgart (1974).

Robertson, Terence, *The Golden Horseshoe*, Evans Brothers Ltd, London (1955).

Rosignoli, Guido, *Ribbons of Orders, Decorations and Medals*, Blandford Press, Poole, Dorset, UK (1976).

Rudel, Hans-Ulrich, *Stuka Pilot*, Euphorion Books (1952).

Schneider, Jost, *Their Honor was Loyalty*, Bender Publications, San Jose, USA (1977).

Schneider, Louis, *Das Buch des Eisernen Kreuzes*, Die Ordens Sammlung, Berlin (1971).

von Seemen, Gerhard, *Die Ritterkreuzträger*, Podzun-Pallas Verlag, Freiburg (1976).

Showell, Jak P M, *U-Boats under the Swastika*, Ian Allan Ltd, Shepperton, (1973).

Showell, Jak P M, *The German Navy in World War Two*, Arms & Armour Press, London (1979).

Toland, John, *Hitler* Doubleday and Company (1976).

INDEX

References to illustrations are in *italic*.